THE MEDIA, THE MESSAGE, AND MAN

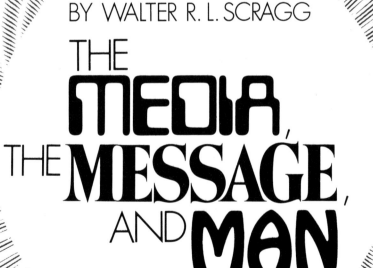

BY WALTER R. L. SCRAGG

THE MEDIA, THE MESSAGE, AND MAN

COMMUNICATING GOD'S LOVE

Southern Publishing Association, Nashville, Tennessee

Copyright © 1972 by
Southern Publishing Association
Library of Congress
Catalog Card No. 72-96066
SBN 8127-0069-4

This book was
Edited by Gerald Wheeler
Designed by Dean Tucker

Text set in 10/11½ Times Roman
Printed on Trade Litho Hibulk
Cover: Scott Mobile C1S

Printed in U.S.A.

DEDICATION

TO MY FATHER

ACKNOWLEDGMENTS

The majority of the Bible references in this volume are taken from The New English Bible. Copyright, The Delegates of the Oxford University Press and The Syndics of the Cambridge University Press, 1961, 1970. Reprinted by permission.

Other translations of the Bible used include:

Revised Standard Version.

King James Version.

The Revised Version.

The New Testament in Modern English. Copyright, J. B. Phillips, 1958. Used by permission of The Macmillan Company.

CONTENTS

Chapter 1

THE LIFE THAT COMMUNICATES

We might as well have been aliens from outer space. Worlds of education, culture, language, technology separated the pygmy tribespeople from us four Australians. How could we bridge the gulf when every gesture, every word, our clothes, their painted bodies—all displayed the complete lack of common ground?

I was a visitor, my three friends missionaries. In a few days we would hold the first camp meeting and the first baptism among these New Guinea clans. When we had stepped out of the twin-engine Piper Aztec plane, tiny naked bodies, each hand clutching an ax or a bow, had instantly surrounded us.

I glanced at my friends. They were smiling and offering the traditional tokens of friendship by hand and voice. Then John's eyes appeared to focus on one person. I followed his gaze. He had found a friend among the crowd. They started toward each other. For a moment the incongruity of their meeting filled my thoughts. Towering above the crowd stood John union mission secretary-treasurer, skilled accountant, college graduate, his mind the fruit of two thousand years of Western thought and Christian heritage. John—who knew how to take excellent photographs, who could speak several languages. Moving toward him was his friend, black teeth stained with betel nut juice, wearing a cloak of beaten bark, a garment of grass around his thighs, a bow in his hand. The little man, product of a strange culture, already physically old though scarcely forty, completely unaware of cars and elevators, of typewriters and supermarkets. How could their minds meet?

A few strides and they were together, dark and white bodies embracing. Red betel nut stained the white shirt. Smiles spoke friendship. In my thoughts the words of the Bible overlaid the rapidly changing scene. "God is love; he who dwells in love is dwelling in God, and God in him." "There is no room for fear in love; perfect love banishes fear." 1 John 4:16, 18. Love had leaped the gap between differing cultures.

For the Christian, love is both the motive and the method of communication. Conscious of what it cost for Heaven to transmit salvation to him, the true believer will seek to convey his knowledge of it through the love that he himself knows. "It is God's purpose to manifest through His people the principles of His kingdom. That in life and character they may reveal these principles, He desires to separate them from the customs, habits, and practices of the world."—Ellen G. White, *Testimonies,* Vol. 6, p. 9.

In a world where the communication explosion titillates the senses of some, distracts others, and confuses still more, a life in constant touch with the Divine speaks most effectively of God's power.

At the same time as the believer instructs others through his life and example, a vast and bewildering stream of impressions bombards him from the unconverted world around him. We all know how such influences can threaten faith and destroy evangelistic zeal. This book seeks God as the Great Communicator in an increasingly complex and technical society.

The Letter

As Paul looked for a way to show the importance of Christian witness and example, he called the Corinthian Christians "epistles" or letters. A modern Paul might speak of his church as a television program, a film, a long-playing record, a cassette. What do others see, read, or hear as our life plays out before them? How clearly do our lives speak of the One whom we profess to serve?

"The world has need of more legible Christians. The language of a Christlike life is intended for all mankind."—*S.D.A. Bible Commentary*, Vol. 6, pp. 843, 844. Every film has its producer and director. Watching a television program, we seldom bother to note who put it together—made it a success or a failure. Yet someone shaped the plot, directed the participants, provided the sets and the equipment. Such people count it an honor to have their names on the credit lines of a film or videotape. Through His Spirit, Christ directs and produces the life of the Christian. Putting us on the air every day, He calls the scene changes and directs how we act.

"The Holy Spirit has been prevented from coming in to mold and fashion heart and mind, because men suppose that they understand best how to form their own characters. . . . But there is only one model after which human character is to be formed—the character of Christ. Those who behold the Saviour are changed from glory to greater glory."—Ellen G. White in *Ibid.*, p. 1098.

The key word for the Ten Commandments in the Old Testament is *eduth*, a "testimony," or "witness." It first appears in Exodus 16:34 when instruction came to place the jar of manna before the "Testimony" in the ark. Later it gave its name to many of the central features of Jewish worship. Thus we read of the "tables of testimony" containing the Ten Commandments, "the ark of testimony," "the veil of the testimony," "the tabernacle of testimony." Why did the commandments give their special name to the major features of the sanctuary? Simply because God displays His character in the Ten. In them He contrasts divine holiness with human weakness. The Spirit can as effectively transcribe God's character on our lives, as the finger of God wrote it on stone. And what He has written proclaims God's character to others and stands as a testimony to Him.

When Israel agreed to the covenant God commanded at Sinai, they were inviting God to write His commandments on their lives. "What then, O Israel, does the Lord your God ask of you? Only to fear the Lord your God, to conform to all his ways, to love him and to serve him with all your heart and soul." Deuteronomy 10:12. Were they to do so in their own strength? "Truly he loves his people and blesses his saints." Deuteronomy 33:3. God would enable them to live up to what He expected.

When the Spirit writes, He does so without falsehood or deception. Under the control of Christ, the life plays true to its divine script. All of us have many audiences before whom we display our life. Our families, our communities, our business associates, our fellow church members, strangers of chance meetings—all tune in to our lives, some for shorter, some for longer periods. "Every thought, every word, and every action of the workers should be of that elevated character which is in harmony with the sacred truth they advocate."—*Testimonies,* Vol. 5, p. 594.

The Widening Circle

What happens at the center affects the rim.

Communication is an ongoing continuous act. When two people come within range of each other, communication of some kind takes place. However, it may or may not be effective. A person will say, "I just couldn't get through to him." Or someone may comment, "I didn't even notice him talking to me."

"Communication runs in a circle, with one communicator (whom we will arbitrarily call, the Source) at one point in the circle, and the other (whom we will arbitrarily label, the Receiver) at another point in the circle. Put them at each end of the diameter . . . of the circle, if you like. Think of the parts of the circle between these communicators as the channel along which they communicate their messages or signals—sound waves, light waves, radio waves, et cetera. The senses too."—Gordon M. Hyde, "When Communication Breaks Down," *Review and Herald,* January 13, 1972, p. 17.

When we act as source and send a message of any kind, the receiver will respond in some way. Even his failure to react may constitute a reply to our message. We can never know where an act of communication will have its end, what results it will produce. Then what should we do to improve our communication with others? Whether we communicate with husband, wife, child, neighbor, stranger, individual, or crowd, the principles are the same.

First, make sure that you as the source have nothing in your life or attitudes that would distort the signal. Second, give the message as clearly and completely as possible. Third, adapt what you say to the needs, interests, and capacities of the receiver. Finally, as a Christian, you must continually relate your life and acts to God.

You are at the center of your own circle of communication. You are a source. Perhaps you may think of yourself as being chiefly a receiver, but that is only a part of what God intends. Through the infilling of Christ you become a source. "A testimony from the heart, coming from lips in which is no guile, full of faith and humble trust, though given by a stammering tongue, is accounted of God as precious as gold."— Ellen G. White in *S.D.A. Bible Commentary*, Vol. 6, p. 1091.

We little realize how easily the thinking of others may magnify our small acts. When "Resurrection City" blossomed on the Mall in Washington, D.C., Adventists decided that they must do something to help with the health of the thousands camped there. It seemed a little act to bring in two disaster relief vans and staff them. Yet that small message of love to a relatively small and deprived group of citizens still speaks for Christ, though several years have passed. In a far greater manner the shy hand that dropped two tiny coins in the offering box of Herod's temple has given a message of sacrifice that will widen its circle through eternity.

The print and broadcast media remind us how easily a small deed may assume prominence. But more than that, while they bring the world to us, they may also take us to the world. Christ told us to love our neighbors. The television set introduces us to neighbors in Pakistan, in Nigeria, in Chile, in Bangladesh. How shall we relate to *their* needs? Individually we cannot answer all of them. Then we must see that the members of a church or group of churches cooperate so that they can take care of the problems. Since we cannot know all men and their difficulties, we must empower those who are on the spot and can offer help. And because we cannot afford to take all the time that it would require to preach to everybody that we know, we must commission others to spend a larger proportion of their time in evangelism.

The communications media often make us more conscious of distant need than local problems. What should we be saying to our neighbors—the people on the same street, the people in the same city? Adventists frequently abhor the social gospel. But for millions it is the only gospel that will communicate God's love.

"Speak as He would speak, act as He would act. Constantly reveal the sweetness of His character. Reveal that wealth of love which underlies all His teachings and all His dealings with men. The humblest workers, in co-operation with Christ, may touch chords whose vibrations shall ring to the ends of the earth and make melody throughout eternal ages."—Ellen G. White, *The Ministry of Healing*, p. 159.

Those Words

Of all the channels of communication open to us, speech remains the most effective. Tempered with Christ's love, speech has added more to the number of the redeemed than any other means of communication.

Christ's use of words offers us an example. "Never man spake like this man." "The words that I speak unto you, they are spirit, and they are life." "If any man hear my voice."

"Jesus' sincerity was very appealing when He was among men. Nothing was so abhorrent to Him as falsehood, and no other class so stirred His wrath as men who were hypocrites. It was because of Jesus' incorruptible sincerity that we have from His lips such a remarkable outpouring of plain words. He spoke exactly what He meant. What He taught, He was.

16

Not very often does an ordinary man put his whole self into his speech. His words reveal him, but they also conceal him. . . . But not so with Jesus—what He thought, He said; what He felt, He declared."—Paul C. Heubach, *This Is Life*, p. 174.

Dare we follow the Master's example? Yes, if we are truly filled with the love He had. With His sincerity went compassion; with truth walked tenderness; with directness marched discretion; with penetration appeared pity; with power came persuasion. Our speaking must be the same.

"A soul filled with the love of Jesus lends to the words, the manners, the looks, hope, courage and serenity. It reveals the spirit of Christ. It breathes a love which will be reflected. It awakens a desire for a better life; souls ready to faint are strengthened; those struggling against temptation will be fortified and comforted. The words, the expression, the manners throw out a bright ray of sunshine, and leave behind them a clear path toward heaven, the source of all light. . . . The expression of the countenance is itself a mirror of the life within. Jesus desires that we shall become like Himself, filled with tender sympathy, exerting a ministry of love in the small duties of life."—Ellen G. White in *S.D.A. Bible Commentary*, Vol. 3, p. 1156.

You can drive away a pet dog by yelling, "Come here, I love you!" or bring it fawning to your knee by gently saying, "Get out, you miserable cur." To speak in love is the only way to speak God's truth. In fact, it ceases to be true when we shape it with anger or self-centeredness. True words may speak a lie because of the emotion that accompanies them. Yet, no mask of love can transform a lie into truth.

In Touch With Heaven

A Christian's circle of prayer embraces many people, many situations. Through prayer we intertwine them with God. Prayer has power because we involve Omnipotence with our own needs and the needs of others.

Surely prayer is the supreme communicative act. Prayer

says God is accessible. "So now, my friends, the blood of Jesus makes us free to enter boldly into the sanctuary by the new, living way which he has opened for us through the curtain, the way of his flesh." Hebrews 10:19. Not only is God accessible, but He is available; not only available, but attentive; not only attentive, but active in our behalf.

We might think of prayer as a triangle that involves us with the Eternal. We talk to God and become one corner of the triangle. When we mention a specific individual, or need, he or it becomes another corner of the triangle. God, at the apex, sees both the object or person for whom we pray and us in our act of prayer. Because He sees and knows both the one who pleads and the one pleaded for, God can both move us in the direction of His will for the other person or object, and guide the other toward Himself.

From the General Conference headquarters in Washington, D.C., an operator types a message to the South American or Trans-Africa Division office, and the message spills instantly from their Teletype. Yet prayer outstrips man's best communications tools. How far away is Heaven? Ten light years? a hundred? or a thousand? Daniel prayed, God heard, and an angel reached his side before the prophet had finished his petition. We can, in our imagination, span vast distances instantly. Does prayer work in a similar way? Is God in instant touch with our thoughts? The Bible implies so.

"Live in contact with the living Christ, and He will hold you firmly by a hand that will never let go. Know and believe the love that God has to us, and you are secure; that love is a fortress impregnable to all the delusions and assaults of Satan. 'The name of the Lord is a strong tower: the righteous runneth into it, and is safe.' Proverbs 18:10."—Ellen G. White, *Thoughts From the Mount of Blessing*, p. 119.

The power that resides in prayer belongs to God's children. When you use prayer, you employ a unique possession of the people of faith. Prayer permits divine love and human need to match orbits and interlock. Then the Holy Spirit boosts us along the trajectory that marks God's will for our lives.

18

Whom God Blesses

Those whom royalty selects to knight or award distinctions to, it greets with the words, "Whom the Queen delights to honour . . ." God also delights to bless His chosen ones. While we should not equate wealth or the lack of it with God's blessing, they are divine gifts. God has spoken to us through lands and possessions. Sometimes we do not hear what God is saying, and, like the parable of the man with the surplus grain, we simply reinvest in more lucrative markets or bonds, or buy more land or a new house.

In Israel's society the rich could easily measure their wealth against the poverty of others. In many cases they knew exactly from whom and by what methods they had accumulated wealth. Isaiah's condemnation in chapter 58 relates to those who flaunted their wealth and accepted no responsibility for the poor.

How we use our possessions indicates to others what God has done for us. We say, "Mr. So-and-so still has the first nickel he ever earned." What does it say of our stewardship? We see people whose educational background, cultural heritage, and moral climate have deprived them of incentive or know-how. What does our stewardship say to them?

Again what does money declare to us? Does it speak to us of more property, a new suite of furniture, a bigger bank balance, more investments? What money means to us, how it entices us, is as important as what our use of money reveals to others.

A popular television commercial invited its listeners to "own a piece of the rock." What does the rock provide? Investments in land, steel, housing, etc. Christ reminds us that such a kind of rock is actually only shifting sand. Then He urges us to partake of the living Rock and build our lives on Him. No Christian has the right to feel proud that he owns "a piece of the rock." What we rejoice in is the Rock that incorporates us.

19

The Communicating Man

Kenneth Holland, *These Times* editor, tells the story of Linda Griggs, a seven-year-old lass who sent a question to the famed heart surgeon Dr. Michael DeBakey. "Does a plastic heart have love in it?" she asked.

The doctor replied, "Yes, a plastic heart does have love in it, a very great deal of love.

"The love in a plastic heart is the love of many people who love other people, and don't want them to die.

"So these people work all day and often all night to build a heart that will make people live longer.

"If you can think of how much love there would be in hundreds of hearts, then that is how much love there is in a plastic heart."

How much love do people find in a gesture, a word, a man, a church, a conference, our church teachings? Enough love to make sacrificial Christians of millions? Enough love to enable a gesture to bring Christ to another? Enough love to change a life?

I get excited when I think what might happen if church members really transmitted God's love, if Christ occupied them sufficiently to make the total man a communication of Christ. "I have been crucified with Christ: the life I now live is not my life, but the life which Christ lives in me; and my present bodily life is lived by faith in the Son of God, who loved me and gave himself up for me." Galatians 2:20.

Our love should equip hospitals, build schools, buy medicines, send missionaries. Christ speaks to the world through the love exhibited in the corporate endeavor of the church. He speaks also through every personal act, the way each person lives. The living, speaking, vibrant Christian cannot help but communicate Christ. Revelation 14 speaks of an angel flying in the midst of heaven. The Greek word is *angelos,* meaning "messenger," human or divine. The angel personifies the church in action. And the angel, the church, needs empowering by our communication of divine love.

"In his efforts to reach God's ideal for him, the Christian is to despair of nothing. Moral and spiritual perfection, through the grace and power of Christ, is promised to all. Jesus is the source of power, the fountain of life. . . . In our behalf He sets in operation the all-powerful agencies of heaven. At every step we touch His living power. . . .

"Through prayer, through watchfulness, through growth in knowledge and understanding, they are to be 'strengthened with all might, according to His glorious power.' Thus they are prepared to work for others. It is the Saviour's purpose that human beings, purified and sanctified, shall be His helping hand."—Ellen G. White, *The Acts of the Apostles*, p. 478.

CHAPTER 2

THE CONFUSED RECEIVER

Students of communications describe the plight of man in graphic words. In today's communications explosion he is the prize in a battle for minds, the experimental guinea pig of Madison Avenue. Propaganda tries to flip him off and on like a light switch.

The Suburban Tract family wakens to a clock radio. At that moment the bombardment begins that will pepper each member of the family with more than 40,000 sense impressions before they go to bed for the night. Mother Tract summons the family to breakfast through the house intercom. In each bedroom a television set and a radio offer a choice of audio and visual impressions to dress by. The teen-agers and sub-teens snap into their jeans to the blast of their stereo. The college freshman takes television so much for granted that neither he nor his parents realize that he has spent more time absorbing from the tube than in the classroom.

The day marches by—bedazzled with neon signs, tantalized with the latest style in graphics, controlled by computers, conditioned by billboards, enticed by window displays, seduced by bookstores, and titillated by film ads. Ellen White must surely have had us in mind when she wrote, "Those who would not fall a prey to Satan's devices must guard well the avenues of the soul; they must avoid reading, seeing, or hearing that which will suggest impure thoughts. The mind should not be left to wander at random upon every subject that the adversary of souls may suggest."—*Messages to Young People,* p. 285.

If the day leaves you confused and weary, then that's par for the course. And tomorrow won't improve things. Tomorrow's technical whizzes plan to wire the supermarket, the computer, the bank, the department store together and put the terminals right in your living room. Then we will find ourselves in an even more intricate communications network.

What Would You Hear?

Only the Christian who has learned to monitor carefully the array of sense impressions bombarding him, and has the self-control to blank off those that damage spirituality, can hope to withstand the attacks made on his mind.

The auditory circuits of the central nervous system—the ears—tune us in to a bewildering array of sounds. Cities threaten the hearing of many. *Time* reports that "in the Loop, Chicago's downtown area, tall office buildings contain and amplify urban sounds like echo chambers so that the din occasionally reaches 90 decibels, enough to cause permanent damage to hearing in 10 percent of the people who might be exposed to it for eight hours a day. The slums, with their high population density and aging, ill-maintained automobiles, are often as noisy. Loudest of all is swinging Rush Street, where night after night the go-go clubs and rock bands blare out music measured at more than 115 decibels, the threshold of pain."—*Time,* October 11, 1971, p. 91.

Noise pollution may easily become moral pollution. Personal transistor radios and portable record players force the individual to assess the spiritual impact of what he hears. Through hi-fi sets and public address systems we may actually broadcast sounds that influence others in a dangerous way.

"Satan is using every means to make crime and debasing vice popular. We cannot walk the streets of our cities without encountering flaring notices of crime presented in some novel, or to be acted at some theater. The mind is educated to familiarity with sin. . . . They hear and read so much of debasing crime, that the once tender conscience, which would have recoiled with horror from such scenes, becomes hardened, and they dwell upon these things with greedy interest."—Ellen G. White, *Patriarchs and Prophets,* p. 459.

When Israel finally came the second time to the River Jordan, one might have expected that nothing would delay their entry into Canaan. Yet many found themselves ill-prepared for the seductive temptations of the Vale of Shittim. Across the river from Jericho stood a Canaanite pleasure resort. The sights, sounds, and fleshpots displayed among the pleasant groves and arbors trapped the unwary Hebrews. Many who might have entered Palestine died as punishment for loss of their self-control.

I remember walking with a friend past the busiest intersection in the bustling city of Melbourne, Australia. Suddenly he grabbed my arm and asked, "Do you hear that?" I could hear trams, buses, and countless cars. "Can't you hear that canary?" he pressed. A few moments of concentration and I, too, caught the joyful cadence of a golden warbler perched three stories up in the window of a hotel room.

Only a person with an ear for the good and beautiful could have heard that sound. And only someone who knew the song of the canary could have selected it out of the cacophony that surrounded him. What are you listening for? What have you tuned your ears to accept? Against what standards are you testing the sounds you consciously choose to hear?

As we tune our ears to hear the good, our lives will become more receptive to the voice of God. Christ still says, "When he comes who is the Spirit of truth, he will guide you into all the truth; for he will not speak on his own authority, but will tell only what he hears; and he will make known to you the things that are coming." John 16:13. Among the counsels given to the church of Laodicea is the statement, "Let the listener hear what the Spirit says to the Churches." Revelation 3:22, Phillips.

Window on the World

"You will have to become a faithful sentinel over your eyes, ears, and all your senses if you would control your mind and prevent vain and corrupt thoughts from staining your soul. The power of grace alone can accomplish this most desirable work."—*Testimonies*, Vol. 2, p. 561.

What does the eye bring to the mind? Color, tint, intensity, hue; form, shape, size, texture; distance, height, length, breadth, depth. The eyes and the optic nerves offer the brain countless images every day. Their fantastically keen receptors monitor almost all the body acts, providing signals that help us adjust stride, posture, and muscle tone.

But the eye is not just an organ that helps us adjust ourselves in a physical world. The eye opens the gate to education, religion, philosophy, art, music, science, mathematics. Through the eye Madison Avenue sells the world on countless products. Television, films, audio-visuals, magazines, billboards, and neon signs testify to the strength of the sight in stimulating human thought and motive. No wonder Jesus said, "If therefore thine eye be single, thy whole body shall be full of light." Matthew 6:22, K.J.V.

Perhaps you have walked down one of the streets, now all too common in the cities of the world, where bookshops, newsstands, and theater marquees pander to the senses. Even the local drugstore offers similar fare. No one makes sunglasses strong enough to hide the glare of sin and debauchery. Christ asks us to take desperate measures to prevent the entry of evil into the life through the senses.

"In order for us to reach this high ideal, that which causes the soul to stumble must be sacrificed. It is through the will that sin retains its hold upon us. The surrender of the will is represented as plucking out the eye or cutting off the hand. Often it seems to us that to surrender the will to God is to consent to go through life maimed or crippled. But it is better, says Christ, for self to be maimed, wounded, crippled, if thus you may enter into life. That which you look upon as disaster is the door to highest benefit."—*Thoughts From the Mount of Blessing*, p. 61.

Christ offers the surrendered will freedom from slavery to the senses. Help awaits those who accept the need for monitoring what they read, watch, and view. Into most Christian homes comes a pipeline of mixed slush, immorality, information, and education. It takes more than average strength of purpose to shut off the faucet and block the flood of pollution.

When Christ prayed that His disciples be kept from the evil pervading the world, He was not making an impossible request. We may view only the good even though our surroundings glisten with evil. The collection and classification of orchids has been my hobby since college. Many times I have spotted varieties growing along the roadside even though I was passing by at fifty or sixty miles per hour. My dad used to say that I had "orchid eyes." In turn I have been fascinated by other experts who can spot their specialty when hidden from me. We might ask ourselves, "What have I trained my eyes to recognize? What should I filter out? What should I let in?"

After Peter and John had healed the cripple by the Temple gate, the Jewish authorities arrested them. The Jewish court ordered them to refrain from any further mention of the name of Jesus. "But Peter and John said to them in reply: 'Is it right in God's eyes for us to obey you rather than God? Judge for yourselves. We cannot possibly give up speaking of things we have seen and heard.' " Acts 4:19, 20. No more can we help being changed by what we select for our attention.

Receptacle of the Spirit

Solomon fully explored the senses. "From the joy of divine communion, Solomon turned to find satisfaction in the pleasures of sense."—Ellen G. White, *Prophets and Kings*, p. 76.

If ever a man conjured up the good life, it was Solomon. "I undertook great works; I built myself houses and planted vineyards; I made myself gardens and parks and planted all kinds of fruit-trees in them; I made myself pools of water to irrigate a grove of growing trees; I bought slaves, male and female, and I had my home-born slaves as well; I had possessions, more cattle and flocks than any of my predeces-

26

sors in Jerusalem; I amassed silver and gold also, the treasure of kings and provinces; I acquired singers, men and women, and all that man delights in. I was great, greater than all my predecessors in Jerusalem; and my wisdom stood me in good stead. Whatever my eyes coveted, I refused them nothing, nor did I deny myself any pleasure." Ecclesiastes 2:4-10.

Solomon's conclusion afterwards?—"I saw that everything was emptiness and chasing the wind, of no profit under the sun." Verse 11.

Much of present culture pampers the senses, the sensual man. Some ads invite us to scratch them, thus releasing the aroma of the product they sell. Advertising highlights flavor, texture, feel, fragrance. Best sellers tout the sensual levels toward which carnal humanity may strive. When exciting the senses becomes an end in itself, we abuse their purpose for existence.

If for some reason you haven't quite made it to the level that some seem to have attained in feeling good or in sensory pleasure, society suggests you can always try alcohol, drugs, a piece of real estate, or some other goody that will give the anticipated high.

"Sensuality is the sin of the age. But the religion of Jesus Christ will hold the lines of control over every species of unlawful liberty; the moral powers will hold the lines of control over every thought, word, and action. . . . Not an impure thought will be indulged in, not a word spoken that is approaching to sensuality, not an action that has the least appearance of evil.

"The senses will be guarded."—Ellen G. White, *Medical Ministry,* pp. 142, 143.

"That men may not take time to meditate, Satan leads them into a round of gayety and pleasure-seeking, of eating and drinking. . . . The lust of the flesh, the pride of the eyes, the display of selfishness, the misuse of power, the cruelty, and the force used to cause men to unite with confederacies and unions—binding themselves up in bundles for the burning of the great fires of the last days—all these are the working

27

of Satanic agencies. This round of crime and folly men call 'life.' "—Ellen G. White, *Evangelism*, p. 26.

An Appeal to Our Hearts

Not just information, knowledge, and sensual pleasure flow into the person through the senses. The senses affect the actual nature of the individual, the basic and innermost drives that make up a person. Long after a series of events have impressed themselves on the mind, the brain has the power to mull them over, rearrange their order, exaggerate certain features, leap to imaginative conclusions, even make the senses experience something when there are no external stimuli present.

One terrible example comes to us from before the world began. An angel experienced the throne room of the universe. He heard, saw, and participated in what went on there. From all the other created beings exposed to the same events came praise for God. Not so Lucifer. His imagination took hold of him. He pictured himself enjoying the prerogatives of divinity. Finally his imagination formulated the thought, "I will be like the most High." Reason, emotion—both became distorted under the pressure of imagination. He sought to communicate the results of his imagination, and gave birth to the monster of sin.

Mind, intellect, emotions—all must yield to God's will. Otherwise the sensual will rule the life. Only the will surrendered to God has the power to prevent the senses usurping control of the life. The senses accept good and evil indiscriminately. Experience may help screen out some of the evil, but only Christ in the heart can provide complete protection against the dangers we face.

The best news of all is that we can live victoriously. Slavery to evil ceases when Christ enters. "You are on the spiritual level, if only God's Spirit dwells within you; and if a man does not possess the Spirit of Christ, he is no Christian. But if Christ is dwelling within you, then although the body is a dead thing because you sinned, yet the spirit is life itself because you have been justified. . . . It follows, my friends, that our lower nature has no claim upon us; we are not obliged to live on that level. If you do so, you must die. But if by the Spirit you put to death all the base pursuits of the body, then you will live." Romans 8:9-13.

The Resources of the Mind

In the science labs of leading universities the mind changers are dabbling with the future. "The discoveries of molecular biology may well show the way to a new comprehension; they may make it possible, through genetic engineering, surgery, drug therapy, and electrical stimulation to mold not only the body but also the mind."—*Time,* April 19, 1971, p. 45.

As we think about the effect of the senses on the spiritual life, remember that the mind has an infinite storage capacity. "Montreal Surgeon Wilder Penfield, for example, while performing operations under local anesthesia, by chance found brain sites that when stimulated electrically led one patient to hear an old tune, another to recall an exciting childhood experience in vivid detail, and still another to relive the experience of bearing her baby. Penfield's findings led some scientists to believe that the brain has indelibly recorded every sensation it has ever received and to ask how the recording was made and preserved."—*Ibid.*

If everything we perceive gets transcribed in the brain, then more than ever we need the cleansing, sanctifying power of Jesus to make us free from the past. How often we need to remind ourselves that Christ "is faithful and just to forgive us our sins, and to cleanse us from all unrighteousness." 1 John 1:9, K.J.V. No wonder Paul pleads with us, "I implore you by God's mercy to offer your very selves to him: a living sacrifice, dedicated and fit for his acceptance, the worship offered by mind and heart. Adapt yourselves no longer to the pattern of this present world, but let your minds be remade and your whole nature thus transformed." Romans 12:1, 2.

Science may ponder the possibility of changing man's inner nature. We know for a fact that it does happen. The human mind can yield to the mind of Christ and let Him direct the life into new channels. "If any man be in Christ, he is a new creature." 2 Corinthians 5:17, K.J.V.

And such change is the work of sanctified reason. In fact, accepting the change offered in Christ is the only reasonable, logical thing for man to do. Certainly we have no hope of transforming ourselves, or our fellowman. We cannot turn off hatred, fear, anger, lust, or jealousy. But God can.

"Christ is the wellspring of life. That which many need is to have a clearer knowledge of Him; they need to be patiently and kindly, yet earnestly, taught how the whole being may be thrown open to the healing agencies of heaven. When the sunlight of God's love illuminates the darkened chambers of the soul, restless weariness and dissatisfaction will cease, and satisfying joys will give vigor to the mind and health and energy to the body."—*The Ministry of Healing,* p. 247.

The Whole Man

In giving us our senses God opened to us a wondrous storehouse of beauty and knowledge. In the earth made new we shall use our senses to explore the wonders of salvation and the mysteries of creation. Even now we view at a distance the treasures of the future. "Eye hath not seen, nor ear heard, neither have entered into the heart of man, the things which God hath prepared for them that love him. But God hath revealed them unto us by his Spirit." 1 Corinthians 2:9, 10, K.J.V.

First, though, we must receive the sanctifying strength of Christ in the life. The Christian has the power to know the world as it really is, and also as it will someday be. His awareness tunes in on the spiritual significance of what he perceives. He knows that the sensual delusions of the day indicate the return of Jesus Christ. And he knows that his imagination, his sensory organs must suffer yet more terrible assaults when Satan unleashes his magic and trickery to deceive mankind.

A battle wages for the minds and bodies of mankind. Assaults from the broadcast and print media rampage against the humble follower of Christ.

How can we stand?

Through control. Yes, the Christian needs self-control, thought control, emotional control, mind control—but above all else, Christ control.

How may we find it?

"In my inmost self I delight in the law of God, but I perceive that there is in my bodily members a different law, fighting against the law that my reason approves and making me a prisoner under that law that is in my members, the law of sin. Miserable creature that I am, who is there to rescue me out of this body doomed to death? God alone, through Jesus Christ our Lord!" Romans 7:22-25.

Can Christ keep us pure and true through all the temptations that assail our faith?

"May the God of peace make you holy through and through. May you be kept in soul and mind and body in spotless integrity until the coming of our Lord Jesus Christ. He who calls you is utterly faithful and he will finish what he has set out to do." 1 Thessalonians 5:23, 24, Phillips.

CHAPTER 3

COMMUNICATING GOD'S LOVE

Scorn and disbelief puckered his mouth and narrowed his eyes. Nothing we said could convince him that God would destroy the earth with fire in the last days.

High in the mountains of New Guinea we had called the village people to join us for worship. Our picture roll told the story of Moses and the burning bush, and the lesson from it had been that one day soon God would burn up the world and make it new. We had provided extremely vivid pictures for unsophisticated minds, we thought.

Then why the disbelief?

Each year the old chief gathered his people and burned the mountains. The dried grass blazed rapidly and drove the small mammals and lizards into the eager hands of the tribespeople. It was a time for feasting and merriment. Then the grass grew again as the year went on its cycle. No one had ever yet set the earth itself afire.

How could we remove the skepticism? I watched as the missionary squatted quietly by the side of the chief, Bible in hand. His fingers rested on 2 Peter 3, his words were slow and distinct. Nobody translated for him. He simply read the words from the "Buka Tambu" or Sacred Book.

What could it have been? The sincerity of the voice? The cadence of the words? A subconscious recognition that what the missionary had said could and would come true? The chief's shaggy head began to nod in agreement. The Bible— through the Holy Spirit—had again communicated God's truth to an unbelieving mind.

When sin erected its barrier in the Garden of Eden, God knew what it meant as a communications problem. To com-

municate face-to-face as He had previously done might well
destroy or at the very least completely overpower the pair.
Yet He must get through to them. He must do something
to redeem the beautiful world that He had created. Somehow
He must make His message so plain that the fallen race could
recognize it and follow it. God had a solution.

"Adam, in his innocence, had enjoyed open communion
with his Maker; but sin brought separation between God and
man, and the atonement of Christ alone could span the abyss,
and make possible the communication of blessing or salvation
from heaven to earth. Man was still cut off from direct approach to his Creator, but God would communicate with him
through Christ and angels."—*Patriarchs and Prophets*, p. 67.

What God Wants to Say

God wants us to know who He is and what He is like.
Satan distorted the truth about God both in heaven and on
earth. "To dispute the supremacy of the Son of God, thus
impeaching the wisdom and love of the Creator, had become
the purpose of this prince of angels."—*Ibid.*, p. 36. Far more
significant than the veil of leaves needed to hide Adam and
Eve from each other and from God was the veil of false
information and fear that sin dropped over the erring pair.

Yet God comes again and again with word of His love
and concern. Even through the tangled, dense web of doubt
and discouragement we discern His love. He wants us to know
that a way stretches from our present need to a future life
paralleling and even surpassing Eden in beauty and happiness.
To point out that way, God has used His own voice, His
finger, nature, prayer, the Holy Spirit, angels, and men whom
He could trust to reveal glimpses of His power and love.

As we watch television, as we listen to the radio, we notice
the same advertisements over and over again. It may take
as many as five distinct and separate media to put a message
across. Acting on the advice of professional Adventist advertising experts, church leaders decided to use several media

in seeking to inform the general public of Mission '72's "Reach Out for Life" campaign. Magazine advertisements, radio and television spots, billboards, bumper strips, and handbills played their respective roles. Any serious advertiser must be prepared to spend extensively to penetrate his market.

Consider the ways God uses to reach us. Think of the price He paid to penetrate personally into our world and convince us of our need and His capacity to fill that need. "Yet on himself he bore our sufferings, our torments he endured, while we counted him smitten by God, struck down by disease and misery; but he was pierced for our transgressions, tortured for our iniquities; the chastisement he bore is health for us and by his scourging we are healed." Isaiah 53:4, 5.

And those who acted as God's messengers paid the price in other ways. "Others, again, had to face jeers and flogging, even fetters and prison bars. They were stoned, they were sawn in two, they were put to the sword, they went about dressed in skins of sheep or goats, in poverty, distress, and misery. They were too good for a world like this." Hebrews 11:36-38.

Yet the cost reveals the value of the purchase. We cannot imagine that God would want to redeem mankind so much that He would commit His own life to the ransom. Yet He was "in Christ, reconciling the world unto himself."

God knows that the communicative acts of His love will succeed. His ways are higher than ours and His thoughts also, and they will not fail. See Isaiah 55:9-11. Yet in a special sense, despite the media of nature, the Holy Spirit, the prophets, even Christ Himself, the extent of God's success depends on the addition of another communicative factor—the witness of our lives filled with Christ's life.

Where Art Thou?

As Source of the message of salvation, God faces a problem of fantastic complexity. You see, you and I, the receivers or potential receivers of His message, have erected shields against it. Some come from our cultural heritage. Others include such attitudes as fear, hate, jealousy, indifference. Satan has his own special array of barriers against God tailored for every individual.

That God succeeds at all in penetrating to us with His message is a tribute to His skill and determination. Once He could talk face-to-face with Adam and Eve. Nothing prevented complete and effective communication. Perhaps the only perfect communications between God and man occurred before the entrance of sin. God as Source can encode the message—putting the message into the proper form to transmit it—but what of our decoding? You can see why it becomes vital that Christ enter our life before we can understand and do God's will. Then God outside us can communicate with God within us (the Holy Spirit).

Countless people have felt cut off from God. Someone has pulled the plug, switched off the set. But that someone is not God. Watch God at work with the faithless couple in the Garden of Eden. They hide and fashion a barrier of leaves. The forest swallows them. In their fear they are us. We identify with them and make our own garments, tread our own dark forests.

"The love and peace which had been theirs was gone, and in its place they felt a sense of sin, a dread of the future, a nakedness of soul. The robe of light which had enshrouded them, now disappeared, and to supply its place they endeavored to fashion for themselves a covering; for they could not, while unclothed, meet the eye of God and holy angels."—*Patriarchs and Prophets,* p. 57.

And where was God?

Where He is today—seeking, calling, communicating His love.

When God asked, "Where are you?" He intended to provoke Adam and Eve into thinking about their condition. God knew where they were. Cut off from face-to-face communication, sinning, dying, their one hope was to realize the position sin had put them in and to accept God's way back.

God did not lose man in the Garden. Man had lost God. The plan of salvation tells how God helped us find Him despite sin.

God Shows Himself

God removed much of the doubt and despair Adam and Eve felt. "Thus were revealed to Adam important events in the history of mankind, from the time when the divine sentence was pronounced in Eden, to the flood, and onward to the first advent of the Son of God. He was shown that while the sacrifice of Christ would be of sufficient value to save the whole world, many would choose a life of sin rather than of repentance and obedience. . . . He trembled at the thought that his sin must shed the blood of the spotless Lamb of God. . . . And he marveled at the infinite goodness that would give such a ransom to save the guilty. A star of hope illumined the dark and terrible future, and relieved it of its utter desolation."—*Ibid.,* pp. 67, 68. *P. P.*

But how could anyone convey and preserve such knowledge? God used the Bible. It contains a record of His acts, His love, His will. "The Lord has preserved this Holy Book by His own miraculous power in its present shape—a chart or guidebook to the human family to show them the way to heaven."—Ellen G. White, *Selected Messages,* Book One, p. 15.

The Bible recounts many meetings between God and man. The Book of Genesis describes God's encounter with Cain. In contrast with Cain who "went out from the Lord's presence," Enoch "walked with God," becoming the first prophet of record. Thus God demonstrated the results of disobedience and obedience. Such stories passed from family to family until the beginning of the written record.

Probably we would have many of the moral and ethical concepts found in the Bible without the written Book. Confucianism, Buddhism, Islam, Hellenistic philosophy all contain the highest morals and ethics. Man by the leading of the

Holy Spirit knows what best suits his condition. Yet just to know such ethical feelings is not enough. Holy Scripture projects the how as well as the what.

The Bible also puts the stamp of divine authority on what a man must do. Mankind cannot know more of God than what he experiences himself. God uses human minds to interpret and express what He is saying. Part of the amazing power of the Bible resides in the wide time and culture spread of its writers. Its remarkable consistency of message carries the impact of inspiration.

We must test what we discover of God within us or through our senses or intellects. To do so, we compare it with what other men have recorded after special, unique acts of communication with God. To the men and women we call prophets God spoke more directly, more concretely than the Holy Spirit does to the rest of us. Their accounts become the objective test we use to make sure we are hearing the Holy Spirit correctly. The Bible, the collection of their writings, becomes "profitable for doctrine, for reproof, for correction, for instruction in righteousness." 2 Timothy 3:16, K.J.V.

By revealing Himself through prophet, priest, and king, God sought to avoid a failing that sin has instilled into the human race. He knew that power-hungry people would manipulate religious communication and knowledge for their own ends. For this reason and others He forbids the use of idols, not even creating a sacred book or manuscript to worship. If you can localize and make an object of the divine, then you can use that object to pressure and force men to your will. All the way from Ephesus to Fatima, from Philistia to Guadeloupe, the evidence is the same. No one must ever "own" God.

The Witness

God wants us to know Him. He recognizes that we know personal beings—our friends, our neighbors, whoever—through relationships. To know someone—to comprehend, to understand what they are and why—we establish a relationship, an involvement with others. Thus God speaks to us in terms of relationships. He taught lessons through His relationship to certain types of sin. Thus He completely destroyed Achan and his family, eliminated Sodom and Gomorrah, and He wiped out the teen-agers who taunted Elisha. We can only understand such events as we grasp what would have been the results if God had let such actions, such sins, reach their ultimate conclusion.

Ellen G. White explains one example. "Had Elisha allowed the mockery to pass unnoticed, he would have continued to be ridiculed and reviled by the rabble, and his mission to instruct and save in a time of grave national peril might have been defeated. This one instance of terrible severity was sufficient to command respect throughout his life. For fifty years he went in and out of the gate of Bethel, and to and fro in the land, from city to city, passing through crowds of idle, rude, dissolute youth; but none mocked him or made light of his qualifications as the prophet of the Most High."—*Prophets and Kings,* p. 236.

In identifying relationships God went to an extreme effort to get our attention and impress us with the importance of what He had to say. At Sinai He put on one of the grandest audio-visual displays the world has yet seen. "On the third day, when morning came, there were peals of thunder and flashes of lightning, dense cloud on the mountain and a loud trumpet blast; the people in the camp were all terrified. Moses brought the people out from the camp to meet God, and they took their stand at the foot of the mountain. Mount Sinai was all smoking because the Lord had come down upon it in fire; the smoke went up like the smoke of a kiln; all the people were terrified, and the sound of the trumpet grew ever louder. Whenever Moses spoke, God answered him in a peal of thunder." Exodus 19:16-19.

Thus with sound and light God gave the Ten Commandments. Forever after the prophets would call the people of Israel back to what God had personally spoken. And to clinch the impact of the Ten, God physically wrote them with His own finger.

No wonder they come to us as the "testimony" or "witness." God revealed His character when He gave the Ten, and He displayed it as a series of relationships between Himself and man, and man with man. The Ten Commandments became known as the "tables of testimony." They gave their name to the ark that contained them, the veil that hid them, and ultimately to the tabernacle itself. Of the three names used to define the Ten in Exodus 34:28, 29—"covenant," "ten commandments," and "testimony"—the Old Testament most frequently used the latter.

For John the Revelator a repetition of the audio-visual display on Mount Sinai immediately followed a vision of the "Ark of the Covenant." When God proclaimed His name again for the Revelator as He had done for Moses, He did it from the "tabernacle of the testimony." (Revelation 15:3-5, K.J.V.) And when God identified His people, He termed them as those who "keep the commandments of God." (Revelation 14:12, K.J.V.)

Finding Inspiration

Some modern theologians suggest that only what we find in the Bible that speaks to us of God is inspired. If a portion of the Bible does not have an impact on us, does not have a message for us, it has no inspiration as far as we are concerned. Others suggest that only certain portions have the value of inspiration. The parts selected for the honor may depend on doctrinal interpretation as with the dispensationalists, or on analysis of language and literary style as with certain Biblical critics.

Fortunately the believer in the Bible has many encouraging evidences that support his trust in Scripture, especially a trust in its accuracy. Archaeology continually pushes us back closer and closer to the original manuscripts of Scripture. The Dead Sea Isaiah scrolls brought us one thousand years closer to the original texts but changed no teachings in the ancient prophet's writings.

Such discoveries are typical of the increasing support for the accuracy of Scripture. Yet the real proof of inspiration comes from our understanding of the nature of God. A personal God who loves must communicate His love to others. We find evidences of such communication both within and outside of ourselves. Holy Scripture, recording the experiences of other believers in God and relaying the divine message, lets us test the validity of our own experience with God.

How did God work through the writers of the Bible? "The Bible is written by inspired men, but it is not God's mode of thought and expression. It is that of humanity. God, as a writer, is not represented. Men will often say such an expression is not like God. But God has not put Himself in words, in logic, in rhetoric, on trial in the Bible. The writers of the Bible were God's penmen, not His pen. Look at the different writers.

"It is not the words of the Bible that are inspired, but the men that were inspired. Inspiration acts not on the man's words or his expressions but on the man himself, who, under the influence of the Holy Ghost, is imbued with thoughts. But the words receive the impress of the individual mind. The divine mind is diffused. The divine mind and will is combined with the human mind and will; thus the utterances of the man are the Word of God."—Ellen G. White in *SDA Bible Commentary,* Vol. 7, pp. 945, 946.

Jesus Christ—God's Total Communication

Lest men have any confusion about His plan, His will, or His person, God sent Himself. "The plan for our redemption was not an afterthought, a plan formulated after the fall of Adam. It was a revelation of 'the mystery which hath been kept in silence through times eternal.' Romans 16:25, R.V. It was an unfolding of the principles that from eternal ages have been the foundation of God's throne. . . . So great was

His love for the world, that He covenanted to give His only-begotten Son, 'that whosoever believeth in Him should not perish, but have everlasting life.' John 3:16, K.J.V."—Ellen G. White, *The Desire of Ages,* p. 22.

Nature had revealed the order and design of the Master for over 4,000 years. For more than 1,500 years a stream of prophets and scribes had written under the inspiration of the Holy Spirit. From the very first that same Spirit had striven with the human race, seeking to make God clear to fallen man. Men could read much of God's will. But it was not enough. "Therein lies the richness of God's free grace lavished upon us, imparting full wisdom and insight. He has made known to us his hidden purpose—such was his will and plea-sure determined beforehand in Christ—to be put into effect when the time was ripe: namely, that the universe, all in heaven and on earth, might be brought into a unity in Christ." Ephesians 1:8-10.

Then if you want to hear God, listen to Christ. If you want to watch Him work, look at the ministry of the Son. If you want to read God, ponder the life of the Saviour. If you want to know His purpose for you, consider what took place on the cross.

John was an old man when he wrote his impressions of his life with the Master, but it was still as vivid as yesterday. He could remember the touch of His hands, the sound of His voice, the tenderness of His eyes, the agony of His death. For John, Christ's whole life showed God communicating. He "heard," "saw," "looked upon," "felt" that life. It became the theme of his ministry.

But God's communication of Christ became something even more. For John it was his "testimony," the center of his thoughts and actions. Only in witnessing to Christ's life could he find satisfaction. "Here is the message we heard from him and pass on to you: God is light, and in him there is no darkness at all." 1 John 1:5. Later John wrote, "God is love." He told us many of the things he learned about God from his time with Christ.

What more can any follower of Jesus do? It is our privilege to adopt the task Paul took to himself. "God . . . chose to reveal his Son to me and through me, in order that I might proclaim him among the Gentiles." Galatians 1:15, 16.

God communicates through Bible, nature, prayer, and experience that we might know Him—and then pass it on.

Chapter 4

THE PROPHETS AMONG US

Early studies in communications theory led some scholars to propose the "Bullet" Theory of communications. "Communication was seen as a magic bullet that transferred ideas or feelings or knowledge or motivations almost automatically from one mind to another. . . . The audience was considered relatively passive and defenseless, and communication could *shoot something into them,* just as an electric circuit could deliver electrons to a light bulb."—Wilbur Schramm and Donald F. Roberts, Eds., *The Process and Effect of Mass Communication,* pp. 8, 9.

But the Bullet Theory didn't hold up. Audiences refused to keel over when ideas hit them. One experiment showed that people with prejudices actually reacted negatively to antiprejudice propaganda and used it to build up their existing prejudices. Audiences shifted ground continually, making themselves no sitting targets.

Current studies in the art of communication have shown that we must take both the source of the message and the receiver into consideration. "We had been concerned with 'getting the message through,' getting it accepted, getting it decoded in approximately the same form as the sender intended—and we had undervalued the activity of the receiver in this process. We had tended to undervalue the importance of the psychological processes that might be triggered by present and stored perceptions of social relationships and role patterns, in such a way as to enter into the response to any communication. Without such complicating concepts we could never explain why the anti-cigarette campaign was not initially more effective, why adoption of new practices proceeds as it does, why violence on television sometimes may and sometimes may not stimulate violence in the behavior of its viewers."—*Ibid.,* p. 11.

What the authors of the previous quotation are trying to tell us is that it is extremely difficult to make communications effective. All of Goebbels' propaganda during World War II, for example, still left many Germans and most Europeans totally unwilling to accept Hitler's Third Reich as the salvation of the world.

You begin to see, then, why God has to be so careful in His message, why He influenced various people in differing circumstances to say the same thing over and over again. And more than that, you begin to see the effectiveness of what God has communicated as you witness its varying acceptance by more than 900 million Christians, both nominal and practicing.

God Finds Men

Communication is something people do. It has no life of its own, does not exist by itself. God communicated with Adam and Eve because a personal relationship demands communication of some kind. Later He established special ties with other people—the holy men of God whom the Holy Spirit motivated. God used them as channels for divine messages to other men. Convinced of the Source of his message, each felt under compulsion to preach it, act it out, teach it, compose it into poems or proverbs, or write it down.

We must not think of the prophets saying to themselves, "How can I communicate God to my people?" Spontaneity marks much of their acts. They move under compelling urgency to convey what they know to be vital. God's communications take on life as people become involved with them. In fact, without such people, God could not have reached mankind as effectively as He did.

Yet, though they probably never wrestled with how they could communicate God, they had self-awareness. A sense

44

of humility, or unworthiness, overcame them as they realized
what God was asking. "Woe is me!" Isaiah exclaims. "I do
not know how to speak," Jeremiah lamented about his inadequacies. The prophets knew that many times people would
completely misunderstand their messages. But they spoke
under the compulsion of the Holy Spirit. Thus, for example,
Zechariah could not refrain from telling his audience, "Last
night I had a vision. I saw a man on a bay horse standing
among the myrtles in a hollow." Zechariah 1:8.

"The Bible, with its God-given truths expressed in the
language of men, presents a union of the divine and the
human. Such a union existed in the nature of Christ, who
was the Son of God and the Son of man. Thus it is true
of the Bible, as it was of Christ, that 'the Word was made
flesh, and dwelt among us.' John 1:14, K.J.V."—Ellen G.
White, *The Great Controversy*, p. vi.

Only in this way can we understand the effectiveness of
the Scripture. In a special sense the prophets had an indwelling
of the Divine. They were God's men, under His guidance
and control. And because they were men, in their writings
we find much with which to identify. They make us sharers
of the Divine that they reveal.

"An earnest, reverent study of the Scriptures, bringing the
mind of the student in direct contact with the infinite mind,
would give to the world men of stronger and more active
intellect, as well as of nobler principle, than has ever resulted
from the ablest training that human philosophy af-
fords."—*Ibid.*, p. 94.

Yet just because the prophets wrote their messages down
does not mean that the Bible will be effective in reaching
people's minds solely by itself. The writing is only half the
story. "The divine inspiration of the Scriptures is not a theory,
but a fact that must be tested on a personal plane. It is not
possible to give a satisfactory explanation of its significance.
As is true with everything that comes from God and relates
to the mysterious work of His Spirit, the inspiration of the
Scriptures infinitely surpasses human understanding. That is

why faith is essential. If explanation were possible, faith in the Bible as the inspired word of God would be unneces- sary."—Jean R. Zurcher, "I Believe . . . in the Bible as the Inspired Word of God," *Review and Herald,* October 14, 1971, p. 5.

One Word

The Bible comes under attack for many reasons. "Some people dismiss the procedure where the Bible is allowed to witness to itself on the basis that it constitutes self-testimony. The argument that the Bible is inspired because it says so is rejected on the ground that such an argument is circular. But this applies no more to the Bible than to any philosophic system or even to geometry. The point is that self-testimony may be true, and therefore must be examined."—John M. Fowler, "Is the Bible the Word of God?" *These Times,* Jan- uary, 1969, pp. 19, 20.

In the Bible God, not man, speaks. Old Testament writers used expressions like: "God said unto me," "Thus saith the Lord God." The New Testament contains the words of Jesus, God the Son. The consistency of the Bible in presenting itself as the Word of God opens it to skepticism. Yet, at the same time, the same claims open to us an avenue to faith. The Bible cannot be a source of great moral truths, a revelation of deity, an expression of infinite love, and be merely the work of mankind.

Its unity supports its claim for divine inspiration. Look at the range of the Biblical writings. Consider the life-styles, the cultures, the educational standards, the wealth of the writers. Examine the different ways in which their thoughts found expression. Such factors should produce contradictions. But in actual fact the Bible remains one whole. "It speaks of one God, uplifts one standard of righteousness, reveals one plan of salvation, and warns of one judgment. In author- ship, in theme, and in purpose the Bible is a single book. No extraordinary committee could have devised such a book.

Only the mastermind of God could make the Scriptures possible."—*Ibid.,* p. 20.

Here are just a few of the unifying concepts of the Bible:

1. Man is sinful and without hope outside of God.

2. God is holy, merciful, and just. God is love and its Source.

3. All need to know the true nature of man and of God.

4. A future life awaits mankind where he will once more share communion with God.

5. Despite his sin, man is of such infinite value that God sent His Son to die for him.

6. Judgment awaits the human race at some future date.

7. All men are equal in the sight of God and deserving of the same opportunities.

The first time I ever heard H. M. S. Richards of the Voice of Prophecy in person, he spoke on the four basic questions that men want answers to. They are: Why am I here? Where did I come from? Who am I? Where am I going? "Answer them," the Voice of Prophecy broadcaster stated, "and you will satisfy the basic need of every man." The Bible answers the questions and so speaks to all. I am here to glorify God and love my neighbor, it declares to us. God made me. I am a son or daughter of God. Christ has promised me eternal life.

The Communicative Gifts

Never forget the role of the receiver in the communications process. Paul suggests that the gifts God gives, properly received, edify the church, build up the ministry, and unite the members.

The gifts of the Spirit are essentially communications gifts. An apostle is one sent, a messenger. Around Christ gathered the twelve disciples. He taught them. But the time came when their role changed. Privileged to witness at first hand the life of Jesus, to hear His message, to watch His death, and to behold Him ascend, they became messengers under the commissioning of the Holy Spirit.

God has never removed the gift of the Holy Spirit from His people. We may see traces of it in an inspiring sermon, article, or other presentation of Biblical truths, a form of the gift we call illumination. If we take from the preacher or writer his work as a teller of God's truth—a duty of the prophet—we diminish his role. Not that he operates at the same level or under the same direction as those inspired of God did, but he does receive a little of the fire that burned on Isaiah's altar.

The evangelist, the pastor, the teacher live among us as evidence of the continuation of the gifts of the Spirit. God sees the Christian as struggling to know, as needing to understand, and as unable by himself to grasp what God is saying. To help us God presented the gifts.

"It is the absence of the Spirit that makes the gospel ministry so powerless. Learning, talent, eloquence, every natural or acquired endowment, may be possessed; but, without the presence of the Spirit of God, no heart will be touched, no sinner won to Christ. On the other hand, if they are connected with Christ, if the gifts of the Spirit are theirs, the poorest and most ignorant of His disciples will have a power that will tell upon hearts. God makes them channels for the outflowing of the highest influence in the universe."—*Testimonies,* Vol. 8, pp. 21, 22.

Where are the gifts today? Perhaps we narrow our vision too much. New communicative gifts continue to offer themselves to the church. Right now the population of the world grows at a rate that exceeds two new people for each of your heartbeats. The old gifts do not suffice. Has the Holy Spirit fallen behind the times? Of course not. God matches the population explosion with a communications explosion. Perhaps we should have a new prayer for our day—a prayer for writers, editors, journalists, broadcasters, communications engineers, and computer programmers. God has given the commission to spread the gospel to men. For men to accomplish the divine task, God gives them talents and abilities. The church is to "come behind in no gift."

48

Greater Than the Parts

Each of the books of the Bible stands alone as a remarkable document. But the Bible as a whole is far greater than the sum of the parts. Job, for example, makes a fascinating story, but its greatest value probably lies in its explanation of human suffering and how that contributes to our overall understanding of God at work in our lives. Proverbs presents an intriguing array of aphorisms and wise sayings. Yet placed in relation to the rest of the Bible, it takes on far greater significance as a guide to human relationships.

Taken as a whole, the Bible clearly establishes man's need and then provides solutions as timeless as the need. Ellen White lists the following among our needs.

1. The knowledge of God that transforms character.—*Ibid.*, p. 329.

2. Cooperation with Christ's redemptive power.—*Education,* p. 29.

3. Faith in God.—*Testimonies,* Vol. 7, p. 211.

4. A higher, purer life.—*The Acts of the Apostles,* p. 478.

5. Baptism by the Spirit.—*Testimonies,* Vol. 5, p. 555.

6. Revival of true godliness.—*Selected Messages,* Book One, p. 121.

7. Revelation or displaying of Christ in His people.—*Testimonies to Ministers,* p. 458.

How could we satisfy such needs without the Word of God to reveal the promised solutions He has made?

The Bible also relates to human problems of many varieties. How more relevant could a book be about the moral plight of society than Paul's counsel that "fornication and indecency of any kind, or ruthless greed, must not be so much as mentioned among you, as befits the people of God. No coarse, stupid, or flippant talk; these things are out of place; you should rather be thanking God. For be very sure of this: no one given to fornication or indecency, or the greed which makes an idol of gain, has any share in the kingdom of Christ

and of God." Ephesians 5:3-5. Some may not like its directness, but no one could deny the relevancy of the statement.

Because the Bible speaks so directly, people try to subvert
its message, to nullify or distort its impact. In doing so they
put themselves in a grave risk. The Bible is bigger than its
moral commands. "Thy word is truth," Jesus said. We deny
our very natures when we deny its principles. Immorality,
degradation, depravity hide the potential in us all. Our true
identity, our complete fulfillment die when we refuse to heed
the Word.

God Speaks Again

Two written testimonies speak to us of God. One is His
holy law which He personally gave, and the other the prophets, men who spoke under inspiration for God. God presented
the Ten Commandments as a witness or outline of His nature.
And at the heart of the Ten He put the Sabbath—a declaration
of His authority and power.

The second testimony, that of the prophets, joins the Ten
in showing the nature and character of God. Among God's
people of the last days the testimony of the Ten will join
the testimony of the prophets. God has restored to His people
both the Ten Commandment law and the "testimony of Jesus
Christ." (Revelation 12:17, K.J.V.)

Terrible apostasy will captivate the world of sin in its last
days. Satan knows he has only a "short time" before his
destruction. Working furiously through false miracles and
counterfeit teachings, he seeks to delude both God's people
and the whole world. Revelation 11 to 14 lifts the lid off
the workings of the devil. God's truth encounters fearful
opposition and His people face fierce persecution as Satan
makes one last, violent thrust against God.

Listen to Satan's frantic attempts to deceive: "Fearful sights
of a supernatural character will soon be revealed in the heav-
ens, in token of the power of miracle-working demons. The
spirits of devils will go forth to the kings of the earth and

to the whole world, to fasten them in deception, and urge them on to unite with Satan in his last struggle against the government of heaven. By these agencies, rulers and subjects will be alike deceived. Persons will arise pretending to be Christ Himself, and claiming the title and worship which belong to the world's Redeemer. They will perform wonderful miracles of healing, and will profess to have revelations from heaven contradicting the testimony of the Scriptures."—*The Great Controversy,* p. 624.

Consider the task of communicating an unpopular message to "every nation, and kindred, and tongue, and people," and you have the reason why God restored the Spirit's gift of prophecy to the church. We might well ask, Where would we be today without the writings of Ellen White?

Testing the Signals

Every broadcasting station must possess an array of testing devices. Most of them determine whether the source of transmission or recording is performing at its best. Noise, flutter, wow, distortion, and a host of other telltale signs indicate faulty equipment. The various meters, gauges, and dials help keep the signals on the right frequency.

In the last days increasing problems will handicap those seeking for religious truth. More and more "evidence" will seem to bring into question the teaching of God's word. More and more delusions will draw people away from the principles of righteousness. Assaults will develop from within and without the church.

"The people of God are directed to the Scriptures as their safeguard against the influence of false teachers and the delusive power of spirits of darkness. Satan employs every possible device to prevent men from obtaining a knowledge of the Bible; for its plain utterances reveal his deceptions. . . . None but those who have fortified the mind with the truths of the Bible will stand through the last great conflict."—*Ibid.,* pp. 593, 594.

THE MEDIA, THE MESSAGE, AND MAN

What weapons does Satan use to assail our faith? Beware
of the new idols of the last decades of the twentieth century—materialism, pride of learning, sophistry, indifference,
and disillusionment. Beware also of the offshoots of modern
theology—subjective standards, "God-is-deadism," new morality, and ecumenism. And finally beware of spurious Adventism—"the Lord delays," fanaticism, and halfway commit-
ment.

More ways exist to deceive the human mind than we dream
of. The Bible lists such ones as:

"They did not open their minds to love of the truth." 2
Thessalonians 2:10.

"Make sinfulness their deliberate choice." Verse 12.

"Give their minds to subversive doctrines." 1 Timothy 4:1.

"Men will love nothing but money and self." 2 Timothy
3:2.

"They will be men who put pleasure in the place of God."
Verse 4.

"Minds be dulled by dissipation and drunkenness and
worldly cares." Luke 21:34.

"Men who scoff at religion and live self-indulgent lives."
2 Peter 3:3.

The answer to the delusions of the last days? The Bible
counsels:

"Find salvation in the Spirit that consecrates you, and in
the truth that you believe." 2 Thessalonians 2:13.

"Possess for your own the splendour of our Lord Jesus
Christ." Verse 14.

"Keep yourself in training for the practice of religion." 1
Timothy 4:7.

"Stand by the truths you have learned and are assured
of." 2 Timothy 3:14.

"Inspired scripture has its use for teaching the truth and
refuting error." Verse 16.

"Be on the alert, praying at all times for strength to pass
safely through all these imminent troubles and to stand in
the presence of the Son of Man." Luke 21:36.

"With this to look forward to, do your utmost to be found at peace with him, unblemished and above reproach in his sight." 2 Peter 3:14.

"Jesus gained the victory through submission and faith in God, and by the apostle He says to us, 'Submit yourselves therefore to God. Resist the devil, and he will flee from you. Draw nigh to God, and he will draw nigh to you.' James 4:7, 8, K.J.V. We cannot save ourselves from the tempter's power; he has conquered humanity, and when we try to stand in our own strength, we shall become a prey to his devices; but 'the name of the Lord is a strong tower: the righteous runneth into it, and is safe.' Proverbs 18:10, K.J.V. Satan trembles and flees before the weakest soul who finds refuge in that mighty name."—*The Desire of Ages,* pp. 130, 131.

CHAPTER 5

CHRIST THE COMMUNICATION

The Bible attaches great significance to names. Often Bible personalities selected their names to describe an encounter with God. Parents expressed their spiritual longings through the names they gave children.

The Son of God's names array before us different aspects of Christ's ministry. In His names and titles you may read what God was saying about Himself, or what the Bible writers saw revealed of God. Thus to the nation of Judah, Isaiah saw Christ as Counselor, Prince of Peace, Wonderful, the Everlasting Father, Mighty God—all names that applied to the people's spiritual condition and needs.

In the New Testament, Christ is Emmanuel, Saviour, Lord, Master, Son of God, Son of man, Lamb of God, King of kings, Lord of lords. Sometimes Christ takes an impersonal name. Thus He comes to us as the Word of life, the Bread of life, the Water of life—figurative names that again show us what we may expect from God as we see Him in Christ.

One of the Bible writers saw Christ especially as the Communication of God to man. John writes of Him as "the Word," or, in the Greek, *logos*. In this name God summarizes one great reason for Christ's coming. The Son came so that we might read God, see Him, know Him. Because He is God, we know the Godhead through Him. Both medium and message, He carried God with Him and showed us how we might be reconciled to the heavenly Father.

In a little town in southern India I saw a juggernaut—a carriage of the gods. At times of festival the priests and their followers mount their god on the heavy, wheeled vehicle. Men push and pull the carriage amid dancing and music. Some-

54

times the frenzy of the fanatics drives them to the supreme act of devotion. They deliberately throw themselves under the rough wooden wheels which crush them to death. And the juggernaut rolls on, oblivious of them. Man has no importance.

How different the message that Christ brought us about God. God is our Father, God is love, God is willing to become the Lamb of sacrifice. He dies under the fearful juggernaut of sin, but man lives because of His death. Christ reveals through His death the worth of the human soul.

Spirit and Life

Many perplexed people listened to Jesus as He told them that they must "eat the flesh of the Son of Man and drink his blood." (John 6:53.) Then Jesus went on to say that His words are "spirit and life." What did He mean?

"Christ used the figure of eating and drinking to represent that nearness to Him which all must have who are at last partakers with Him in His glory. . . . As we believe and receive the words of the Lord Jesus, they become a part of our spiritual life, bringing light and peace, hope and joy, and strengthening the soul as physical food strengthens the body."—Ellen G. White in *S.D.A. Bible Commentary,* Vol. 5, p. 1135.

"We eat Christ's flesh and drink His blood when by faith we lay hold upon Him as our Saviour."—*Ibid.*

"In our daily lives, before our brethren and before the world, we are to be living interpreters of the Scriptures, doing honor to Christ by revealing His meekness and His lowliness of heart. Christ's teachings are to be to us as the leaves of the tree of life. As we eat and digest the bread of life, we shall reveal a symmetrical character. By our unity, by esteeming others better than ourselves, we are to bear to the world a living testimony of the power of the truth."—*Ibid.*

Christ is both the Word and the source of words. He lived as God among us, and taught us the words of life. Peter said Christ possessed the "words of eternal life." Power resides in them. What would happen to us if we really believed His words and let them loose in our lives? What transformations would we see? What concern for others? What a change in the way we live, speak, act?

Primitive societies reveal the power of God's word. In the highlands of New Guinea a few hundred yards will often show the difference. In one village mouths drip betel nut juice, pigs compete with dogs and children for food scraps, a mother suckles a piglet. Fear lurks in everyone's eyes. Strange spirits and lurking terrors people their imaginations. Yet the same people—under the influence of the Word and His words—begin to smile, discover their own and each other's worth, change the status of women and children, clean up their bodies and minds, drive out the ghosts of superstition, rebuild their homes, and change their personal habits. No one who has witnessed such transformations can doubt the power of the Word.

Christ asserted that His authority issued from the Father. His hearers puzzled over the concept that God was among them. For some the idea that the Son of Joseph and Mary was the Word of God lay beyond belief. How could the God the Scriptures taught about come Himself and talk with them? How could a Man, appearing with no blazing light, no crashing thunder, no earthquake, no trumpet blast, be God? Yet those who read Him for what He was, experienced Him personally as the Son of God—the express image of the Father. And right now that same Man still offers us the truth about God.

Making Truth Clear

"When in former times God spoke to our forefathers he spoke in fragmentary and varied fashion through the prophets. But in this final age he has spoken to us in the Son whom he has made heir to the whole universe, and through whom he created all orders of existence: the Son who is the effulgence of God's splendour and the stamp of God's very being, and sustains the universe by his word of power." Hebrews 1:1-3.

Jesus Christ, God incarnate—a concept that often puzzles and sometimes alienates many. Yet the presence of Christ on earth climaxes the logic of Deity. Evidence of Personality pervades the universe. We sense it in order, design, law, and we recognize it from the existence of beauty and reason. Thus God, a personal Being who relates to other personal beings, came among men. He came to fill the vacuum sin has created, to insert Himself into the God-shaped blank that every life possesses, to direct man toward his Creator, and to tell of God.

To think of Christ as less than God, to call Him "great teacher," or "noble mind," or "a divine presence" changes the nature of His mission. "When a man's real belief in Christ consists in regarding Him as leader, hero, the *primus inter pares*, the highest point in the history of religion, the loftiest peak in the moral and religious history of humanity, he would do better, for the sake of simplicity and truth, to renounce the use of the terms Christ, Son of God, Redeemer, Mediator, Reconciler, for all these terms mean something quite different."—Emil Brunner, *The Mediator*, p. 79.*

The names given Jesus upon His incarnation reveal Christ to be not just a representative of God, not merely one showing the value and importance of God, but that He *is* God. Christ is called Jesus or Saviour; Emmanuel, God with us; the Son of God; the Word. Thus God indicates the things He wanted us to discover in Christ—the plan of salvation, God's identity with man's condition, the fatherhood of God, and the true nature of God.

To bring truth alive Christ spoke in parables. Many of the concepts would escape us if we heard only the basic, unadorned, abstract principle. Vivid figures, everyday lan-

---

The Mediator, by Emil Brunner, translated by Olive Wyon. The Westminster Press. Copyright 1947, W. L. Jenkins. Used by permission.

guage, impress His principles on our minds.

"In parables and comparisons He found the best method of communicating divine truth. In simple language, using figures and illustrations drawn from the natural world, He opened spiritual truth to His hearers, and gave expression to precious principles that would have passed from their minds, and left scarcely a trace, had He not connected His words with stirring scenes of life, experience, or nature. . . . In this way He was able to make sufficient impression upon the heart so that afterward His hearers could look upon the thing with which He connected His lesson, and recall the words of the divine Teacher."—Ellen G. White, *Fundamentals of Christian Education,* p. 236.

Christ's parables remain remarkably fresh to our ears. The miracle of the seed still keeps its meaning. We know what it is to lose money and see a child waste his life. The talents demanded in a business-oriented society, and the treatment of the boss's management group are familiar to us. One might think that words spoken to a pastoral society would lose their significance to a technical society. But part of the timelessness and divinity of Christ's teaching lies in His choice of figures and parables.

Empathy and Sympathy

Our Lord did more than just theoretically understand the burdens and sorrows of others. Experiencing these burdens with them, He could *sym*pathize as well as *em*pathize. He knew the yearning of blind Bartimaeus more than just as an impartial observer of human suffering. Christ entered the mind and heart of the poor man and felt the intensity of his need, the misery of his condition. Jesus measured the bitterness and heartache of the woman who reached to touch Him in the crowd. He felt her weakness and longing.

The word *compassion* means "feeling with." When Jesus wept at the grave of Lazarus, it was because He shared the intense sorrow of those who loved the dead man. "Yet on himself he bore our sufferings, our torments he endured, . . . he was pierced for our transgressions, tortured for our iniquities. . . . The Lord laid upon him the guilt of us all." Isaiah 53:4-6.

The exhausted Saviour who seeks a mountain retreat, the tireless treating of the sick, the miles trudged from village to village, the tears over Jerusalem, the desperate agony of Gethsemane show what it means to bear the name "God with us." They say to us that God knows, He sees, He cares. Peter knew it when he said, "Cast all your cares on him, for you are his charge." 1 Peter 5:7.

Watching a stream of busy ants moving from food to nest shows tireless activity, apparent order, group activity—at least we think it does. We can know nothing of the drives and instincts that accomplish so much. In fact, watching one ant busy on the trail, and lifting our eyes for just one moment, may make it impossible for us to identify that ant again. They all look the same, as if some plastic molder had stamped them out with machined precision. They do not vary in color or shape. Nothing sets off or individualizes one ant from another.

Too often Christians develop an ant complex. They think God does not know about them, that He must be off caring for the big problems. As a result they feel like ants—busy, remote, and lost in a crowd. Christ brought with Him the message that we need not be someone special to qualify for divine attention. "Thou God seest me," applied to the multitude as well as to Moses, to the little children as well as great Solomon.

Francis Thompson, an English poet, sought to express God's concern for him, individually, in a poem called, "The Hound of Heaven." In it he describes his experience as of an animal tracked tirelessly by a hunting dog. Nowhere could he hide from the divine Hunter. Though he fled from Him through days and years God was still there, seeking. And if we will just open our eyes, we will find God with us. He is always there, waiting and longing to help.

Sincerity

Christ's teachings have an amazing ability to override the insufficiencies of those that use them. How else could we explain the universal adoption of Christianity by the slaves in the United States and other countries? How else, the continued rebirth of the Christian hope in each succeeding generation, when all too often parents and others have barely followed Christ's teachings? How else, the spread of Christianity as a vital force into many countries despite the ruthless aggression, immorality, and oppression from those who called themselves Christian? The words of Christ are greater than our attempts to emulate them. His teachings and His life challenge us. Each true follower of Jesus sees them as speaking to him, and hope comes alive that one might yet attain to the "measure of the stature of the fulness of Christ," might yet emulate His character.

Jesus appeals to the young and old, regardless of race or creed, because He is no "put on." He is "for real." Complete sincerity comes through in His life and teaching. And not just sincerity, but kindness, love, and courtesy marked the communications of Jesus. He scorned cant and hypocrisy and showed men their real nature.

Jesus reached the woman at the well because He identified with her need, not condemning, but uplifting. And so He does with us all.

"The religion of Christ is sincerity itself. Zeal for God's glory is the motive implanted by the Holy Spirit; and only the effectual working of the Spirit can implant this motive. Only the power of God can banish self-seeking and hypocrisy. This change is the sign of His working. When the faith we accept destroys selfishness and pretense, when it leads us to seek God's glory and not our own, we may know that it is of the right order."—*The Desire of Ages,* p. 409. Jesus showed us selflessness by declaring that He had come to do the will of the Father, and by offering Himself as a servant of mankind. Sincerity is not just words, it is a way of life.

For years now the mass media have informed us insistently that a certain beverage is "the real thing." A "sincere" drink, perhaps? And more of the carbonated drink sells than any other soda. People crave the genuine. The eternal search for reality, for quality, motivates many commercial ventures. The Christian's search for the real thing leads inevitably to Jesus. Paul could invite his readers to do what he said, what he taught, and what he did, because his words tallied with his acts. Christ's penetration of his life-style made him so much like the Master that the church could safely pattern after him.

God unveiled Himself in the Son. When we show Christlike characteristics, we also unveil God to friends, neighbors, loved ones.

"It is the Holy Spirit, the Comforter, which Jesus said He would send into the world, that changes our character into the image of Christ; and when this is accomplished, we reflect, as in a mirror, the glory of the Lord. That is, the character of the one who thus beholds Christ is so like His, that one looking at him sees Christ's own character shining out as from a mirror. Imperceptibly to ourselves we are changed day by day from our own ways and will into the ways and will of Christ, into the loveliness of His character. Thus we grow up into Christ, and unconsciously reflect His image. . . . To be a Christian is to be Christlike."—Ellen G. White in *S.D.A. Bible Commentary,* Vol. 6, p. 1097.

Christ—Word of God

"The Prologue to John's Gospel is the profoundest piece of writing in all literature. It opens with the words: 'In the beginning was the Word, and the Word was with God, and the Word was God.' It has been stated that John derived his doctrine of the Logos from Philo, the Jewish-Alexandrian philosopher, who developed a speculative doctrine of the Logos. But in John the Logos is Personal, Eternal, Divine,

61

Human, Creative, Light-producing, and Life-possessing. All this, which is God's unveiling of His Son through John, is far in advance of anything that Philo ever wrote. . . . Christ is the eternal Word, the One in whom God has unfolded His Eternal Purpose, manifested His Wonderful Love, and disclosed His Innermost Thought."—Robert Clarke, *The Christ of God,* pp. 6, 7.

From the Word of life comes the "common life, that life which we share with the Father and his Son Jesus Christ." 1 John 1:3. From Christ came "the message . . . that God is light, and in him there is no darkness at all." Verse 5. We know Christ when "we keep his commands." 1 John 2:3. Because Christ came, "darkness is passing and the real light already shines." Verse 8. "To deny the Son is to be without the Father; to acknowledge the Son is to have the Father too." Verse 23. Through the Word we know that "love must not be a matter of words or talk; it must be genuine, and show itself in action." 1 John 3:18. Through Christ God's "love was disclosed to us in this, that he sent his only Son into the world to bring us life." 1 John 4:9. From Christ Himself came the command, "that he who loves God must also love his brother." Verse 21. The greatest witness to the Sonship of Christ is, "that God has given us eternal life, and that this life is found in his Son." 1 John 5:11. Only God can give eternal life.

John knew much from personal experience. He wrote as a firsthand witness to the teachings of Christ. He summed up the words of the Word when he said, "We know that no child of God is a sinner; it is the Son of God who keeps him safe, and the evil one cannot touch him." Verse 18. Thus Christ preserves us from the condemnation due sinners. Second, "We know that we are of God's family, while the whole godless world lies in the power of the evil one." Verse 19. Thus Christ includes us in the sinless family of the universe. Third, "We know that the Son of God has come and given us understanding to know him who is real; indeed we are in him who is real, since we are in his Son Jesus Christ. This is the true God, this is eternal life." Verse 20. Thus Christ includes us in the immortality that flows from God.

Eternal Truths

"A man who was merely a man and said the sort of things Jesus said would not be a great moral teacher. He would either be a lunatic—on a level with the man who says he is a poached egg—or else he would be the Devil of Hell. You must make your choice. Either this man was, and is, the Son of God: or else a madman or something worse. You can shut Him up for a fool, you can spit at Him and kill Him as a demon; or you can fall at His feet and call Him Lord and God. But let us not come with any patronising nonsense about His being a great human teacher. He has not left that open to us. He did not intend to."—C. S. Lewis, *Mere Christianity*, pp. 52, 53.

Four great teachers come to us from the ancient past, each of whom has left an indelible mark on the thinking of the human race: Zoroaster, Buddha, Socrates, and Mohammed.

Zoroaster, a Persian of the sixth century before Christ, opposed polytheism and converted to the sole worship of Ahura Mazda when thirty. While he would place curses on his opponents, he believed that material prosperity and godliness went hand in hand.

Buddha, born shortly before Zoroaster died, became the Enlightened One and proposed a philosophy he called the Middle Way of the eight-fold path. He emphasized moralistic concepts and rejected his native Hinduism and the Hindu gods.

Socrates was born shortly after Buddha died. The Delphic Oracle proclaimed him the wisest man on earth. He tried by questions to prove it untrue. Finally his followers accused him of pederasty and actually helped condemn him.

Mohammed claimed to have received a vision from Allah at forty. He taught uncompromising monotheism, prayer five times a day, fasting for a month each year, and pilgrimage to Mecca. See Edwin M. Yamauchi, "Historical Notes on the (In)comparable Christ," *Christianity Today*, October 22, 1971, pp. 7-11.

How does Christ differ from these great teachers? "To maintain that all these leaders are equivalent is to argue not from tolerance but from ignorance."—*Ibid.*, p. 11. Here are some important distinctions:

1. Jesus was celibate.

2. Only Jesus came from a background that was already monotheistic.

3. His death by crucifixion is unique. "What is so unique about the death of Jesus on the cross is not its manner but its alleged redemptive meaning. The early accounts as opposed to later hagiographical apocrypha do not claim for the other religious founders the ability to redeem men and to forgive their sins."—*Ibid.*

4. Early sources do not attribute miracles to the other four men as they do in the case of Jesus.

5. Only Jesus spoke on His own unquestioned authority.

6. Only the followers of Jesus claimed His resurrection.

7. Only Christ claimed equality with the sole, supreme Deity.

Christ is unique, incomparable, the Word of life, the Word of God.

"Christ was 'God with us.' The light of the knowledge of the glory of God is in the face of Jesus Christ. Without Him we could never know God in the fulness of His love and grace, and without Him we can never see Him in the matchless splendour of His glory."—Robert Clarke, *The Christ of God*, p. 40.

CHAPTER 6

CONTROL CENTRAL

The Holy Spirit came from the Father as Comforter, Paraclete. His presence pervaded the world from before creation. He walked with Enoch, inspired the lyrics of David, rebuked the decadent Solomon, strengthened Daniel's faith, convicted Jonah's mission field of Nineveh. Yet He only appears as Comforter when Christ leaves earth and returns to heaven.

Think of Him as the continuing Presence of the Godhead. Once Christ died, He could assume a universal role, affecting all men and directing them to the plan of God. As Third Person of the Godhead, the Spirit moves through the world with all the powers and prerogatives of Deity. He sees, knows, is. All men receive His attention everywhere. Through Him the redeeming resources of the grace of God appear to all men. Through Him we say, "Thou God seest me."

For the mass of humanity He is the eternal Conscience. Not that He is your conscience, or my conscience, though He may become so. All too often, human consciences distort, sear, harden. Yet the Spirit acts as a universal Personal Force that motivates all men everywhere toward good and away from evil. He makes the rich aware of the poor, the powerful conscious of the weak. The Holy Spirit creates pity for the deprived, the homeless, and the tragedy-stricken. Without Him the world would become worse. God looked at Noah's day and said, "My spirit shall not always strive with man." Genesis 6:3, K.J.V. Our day, so like Noah's, lives under the same awful possibility.

Through Christ's death the Spirit's task as Conscience of the world became potentially more successful. "When he comes, he will confute the world, and show where wrong and right and judgement lie. He will convict them of wrong by their refusal to believe in me; he will convince them that right is on my side, by showing that I go to the Father when I pass from your sight; and he will convince them of divine judgement, by showing that the Prince of this world stands condemned." John 16:8-11.

The Spirit does more than just the work of Conscience in His role of Comforter of God's children. For them He is Advocate and Guide. He communicates truth, represents man before God, leads individuals and the church. "However, when he comes who is the Spirit of truth, he will guide you into all the truth." Verse 13. Responding minds hear the voice of the Spirit and follow Him to truth.

God accomplishes yet more through the Spirit. He is the Spirit of Power. For the church and the Christian in their responsibility to tell the gospel to the world, He is the divine Power Terminal. Only He can supply the strength and impact we need to spread the gospel, the divine current required to operate the machinery of the church. Jesus assured the disciples, "You will receive power when the Holy Spirit comes upon you; and you will bear witness for me in Jerusalem, and all over Judaea and Samaria, and away to the ends of the earth." Acts 1:8.

Finally, the church in the last days looks to the Spirit for a special work that God has promised to accomplish in our midst. He is the Latter Rain, the Refreshing Showers, that endow God's people with the special spiritual strength they need to prepare for the coming of Christ. "Be glad then, ye children of Zion, and rejoice in the Lord your God: for he hath given you the former rain moderately, and he will cause to come down for you the rain, the former rain, and the latter rain in the first month." Joel 2:23, K.J.V.

Guidance System

As the world watched the Apollo lunar landing on television, the small computer brain in the LEM sensed the

66

approaching surface of the moon. Like a skilled pianist it orchestrated the space vehicle's approach, dropping the craft surely and safely to a landing. Yet the relays and switches, the microcircuits and memory cells of the spacecraft computer alone were not enough. Behind that dramatic display of coordination and skill lay a whole bank of computers and thousands of human programmers and operators—the entire staff of mission control in Houston, Texas.

A universe of unfallen beings will rejoice over every soul that follows the orbit of eternal life to the heavenly home. Yet our safe arrival will represent little of our effort. Behind each of the redeemed people of God stands the controlling, guiding, loving presence of the Spirit.

God keeps in continuous communication with the human race through the Holy Spirit. Thus God has never gone away as it might have seemed when Christ returned to heaven. God remains with us as Advocate and Comforter. The Bible reveals the Holy Spirit as far more than a motivating Impulse, or an impersonal Presence. For example, we may grieve Him. It is impossible to grieve, to make sorrowful, an impersonal force. Also He guides and convicts, something conscious beings do best. By giving Him the name Paraclete or Comforter Christ pointed to Him as a person who would take over Christ's role on earth. Because He is a person, He reflects the Godhead by knowing us personally, individually. He can tailor His guidance, His gifts of power, His work of preparation to meet our different needs. But because the Son of God remains Heaven's chosen way of revealing itself to us, we see only occasional glimpses of the unique nature of the Spirit, the Third Person of the Trinity. Christ said, "He shall not speak of himself; but whatsoever he shall hear, that shall he speak: and he will shew you things to come. He shall glorify me: for he shall receive of mine, and shall shew it unto you." John 16:13, 14, R.S.V.

For everyone the Holy Spirit functions as the contact point with Divinity. He uses sorrow, joy, pain, the varying circumstances of life, to point us to God. He functions within the known to reveal the Unknown. Thus He is with the millions of India who live in utter ignorance of Jesus Christ, as much as He is with the sophisticates of Western society who may view Christian faith as superstition. Through Him, God is ever present.

"Although in the depths of heathenism, with no knowledge of the written law of God nor of His Son Jesus, they have revealed in manifold ways the working of a divine power on mind and character. . . . The Holy Spirit is implanting the grace of Christ in the heart of many a noble seeker after truth, quickening his sympathies contrary to his nature, contrary to his former education. . . . Heaven's plan of salvation is broad enough to embrace the whole world. God longs to breathe into prostrate humanity the breath of life. And He will not permit any soul to be disappointed who is sincere in his longing for something higher and nobler than anything the world can offer."—*Prophets and Kings,* pp. 376-378.

Spiritual Sensors

"God has put within each one of us something that cries aloud against us whenever we do that which we know to be wrong. Conscience is the detective that watches the direction of our steps and decries every conscious transgression. Conscience is a vigilant eye before which each imagination, thought, and act is held up for either censure or approval.

"An American Indian once gave the following definition: 'Conscience is a little three-cornered thing inside me. When I do wrong it turns around and hurts me very much, but if I keep on doing wrong it turns so much that the corners come right off and it doesn't hurt me any more.' "—Billy Graham, "The Conscience," *Decision,* March, 1971, p. 12.

Billy Graham says, "I believe there is no greater argument for the existence of God in the world today than conscience."—*Ibid.* He goes on to state, however, that the conscience may become our worst enemy. The conscience must be Spirit-directed if we are to have it take us to eternal life.

Natural man does not recognize the promptings of the Spirit for what they are. He may obey them, but blindly. They may eventually bring him to Christ, but for long years they may seem to him to be no more than moral or ethical longings for a nobler life. History is full of examples of some leader bringing great moral reforms in a pagan culture. Obviously the Holy Spirit influenced such reforms.

Yet, when a person becomes conscious of who it is that is urging him heavenward, when he becomes spiritually aware, then his life changes dramatically. He may struggle with the Spirit, may wrestle with His proddings, may fight against Him, but from that point such a man will never be the same. Should he yield to Christ and accept the Spirit as Advocate and Comforter, then, the Bible says, he may have "the mind of Christ."

To have the mind of Christ is to see with a different vision, march to a different drummer. The natural mind cannot conceive the joys, anticipations, triumphs, and hopes of the follower of Jesus. To him they are foolishness. But the Christian puts out sensors that tap sources of information and light that seem only darkness to the one outside Christ. The natural man cannot "see" heaven or the new earth. He cannot taste the thrill of forgiven sin, the clean-washed feeling of being born again. Yet the Christian knows such joys and rejoices in them.

"Oh, how much we lose by not educating the imagination to dwell upon divine things, rather than upon the earthly! We may give the fullest scope to the imagination, and yet, 'eye hath not seen, nor ear heard, neither have entered into the heart of man, the things which God hath prepared for them that love him.' Fresh wonders will be revealed to the mind the more closely we apply it to divine things. We lose much by not talking more of Jesus and of heaven, the saints' inheritance. The more we contemplate heavenly things, the more new delights we shall see, and the more will our hearts be brimful of thanks to our beneficent Creator."—Ellen G. White in *S.D.A. Bible Commentary*, Vol. 6, p. 1085.

Input-Output

We may well regard the Spirit as the Organizer of the church's activities on earth. Besides being its source of power, He provides the church with the skills needed to meet the demands of the gospel commission.

Most large retail operations use computers to maintain inventories. In some chains the computer adjusts the stock lists as the cash register rings up the sales receipt. Thus the computer printouts permit the business to make readjustment of stocks, movement of staff, supplies, etc.

What is the printout of the church's needs today? Missionaries in New Guinea, a doctor in Africa, a pilot in Brazil, a nurse in Hong Kong, a teacher in India? As we struggle to fill the various positions, the Holy Spirit works with the church, urging, convincing, encouraging, even supplementing human skills. And what of the great need for revival and reformation? We can never be the people God must have, or do the task the times require of us without His influence. "The influence of the Holy Spirit is needed that the work may be properly balanced and that it may move forward solidly in every line."—*Testimonies,* Vol. 6, p. 291.

What prevents the Holy Spirit from complete guidance of the church? Too many of us have let the world assume control of us.

"The intellect is to be kept thoroughly awake with new, earnest, whole-hearted work. How is it to be done? The power of the Holy Spirit must purify the thoughts and cleanse the soul of its moral defilement. . . . The office and work of the Holy Spirit is not for them to use it, as many suppose, but for the Holy Spirit to use them."—*Fundamentals of Christian Education,* p. 227. "The Holy Spirit is not a servant, but a controlling power."—Ellen G. White, *Gospel Workers,* p. 155.

Thus the gifts of the Spirit are not of our choosing, but of the Spirit's giving. He orchestrates surrendered lives according to the needs of God's plan. If more is not done, more gifts not received, then too few instruments have yielded to His baton.

The church has made progress. In 1910 one person in every 13,000 had accepted Seventh-day Adventism. By 1971 the proportion had improved to about 1 to every 2,000. A population explosion saps the resources of the church, but the hidden resources of the Spirit seem hardly tapped.

Remember, "To us today, as verily as to the first disciples, the promise of the Spirit belongs. . . . At this very hour His Spirit and His grace are for all who need them and will take Him at His word. . . . Christ declared that the divine influence of the Spirit was to be with His followers unto the end. But the promise is not appreciated as it should be; and therefore its fulfillment is not seen as it might be. . . . It is the absence of the Spirit that makes the gospel ministry so powerless."—*Testimonies,* Vol. 8, pp. 20, 21.

Course Correction

We arrived late off the reef near Kwailebesi in northern Malaita in the Solomon Islands. Just minutes before, the tropical sun had dipped into a golden ocean, but already darkness hid the shore. Not complete darkness, though. We could all make out the dim light of a kerosene lantern propped on the end of a little coral pier.

Earlier that day the captain had cautiously threaded his way through the reef to Lunga-Lunga. Fearful-looking coral outcroppings had threatened the copper sheathing of our small ship, the *Lao Heni.* Now we must make the same trip by starlight.

Cutting the engine to quarter-speed, we inched toward the reef. Seated on the prow of the motor ship, the captain called direction changes to the helmsman. Time dragged. The light on the pier appeared in first one direction then another. The captain could actually see the reef by the dim light of the lantern. Finally the ship slid in against the pier.

71

Jesus came to put men right with God. Through faith in Him we possess righteousness. But life stretches ahead. The dangers of the past repeat themselves with uncanny frequency. New temptations swirl across our bows. We skirt disaster at every swing of the helm. Yet light glimmers from the heavenly shore. And who is the Captain of our lives? "However, when he comes who is the Spirit of truth, he will guide you into all the truth." John 16:13.

Nicodemus heard words that the spiritual man cherishes. To be born again means to have the Spirit give us new life. Note the spiritual assets that Paul ascribes to the Spirit in Romans 8:

1. The Spirit sets us free from the law of sin and death. Verse 2.

2. He controls our conduct. Verse 4.

3. A spiritual outlook comes through the influence of the Spirit. Verse 6.

4. Christ's indwelling Spirit gives new life to the mortal body. Verse 11.

5. The base drives of the body die with the cooperation of the Spirit. Verse 13.

6. The Spirit testifies that we are children of God. Verse 16.

"The sap of the vine, ascending from the root, is diffused to the branches, sustaining growth and producing blossoms and fruit. So the life-giving power of the Holy Spirit, proceeding from the Saviour, pervades the soul, renews the motives and affections, and brings even the thoughts into obedience to the will of God, enabling the receiver to bear the precious fruit of holy deeds."—*The Acts of the Apostles*, p. 284.

Assured Trajectory

One does not drive a rocket. Instead one aims it along a course called a trajectory. Only rarely do astronauts assume manual control of their craft. Long before they head for the launching pad, scientists have calculated a trajectory for it to follow and will refigure it over and over as needed during the flight. The rocket engines and steering jets fire only for short bursts. Even then the computer controls the situation.

Christians who have yielded themselves to the control of the Spirit find that He has allotted and planned for every need they will have. An off-course Christian has not learned to let the Spirit guide him.

The obstinate sinner who refuses the plan and pardon that God offers blasphemes the Holy Spirit. His refusal insults God's plan. But God does not turn away from him. Jesus stands outside the door, knocking. We have no picture of God turning away from those who want Him near. It is we who walk away from God to find a back room, a hiding place where we cannot hear the persistent knock.

God cannot forgive the sin that we cherish and refuse to confess. Such a sin is an unpardoned sin, because we do not seek pardon. Unpardoned sins grow into the unpardonable sin.

The Holy Spirit acts as the Sealer of God's people. Examining our minds, He computes our loyalties, tests our life direction. As a result He knows "them that are his." Finally, just before the second coming, He acknowledges the faithful children of God by applying the seal, the stamp of His approval.

"Just as soon as the people of God are sealed in their foreheads—it is not any seal or mark that can be seen, but a settling into the truth, both intellectually and spiritually, so they cannot be moved—just as soon as God's people are sealed and prepared for the shaking, it will come."—Ellen G. White in *S.D.A. Bible Commentary,* Vol. 4, p. 1161.

Toward Tranquility Base

God waits to see His character vindicated and duplicated in His people. When that happens, Christ will come. Heaven waits for us to prepare.

Who will be sealed? "God has laid a foundation, and it stands firm, with this inscription: 'The Lord knows his own', and 'Everyone who takes the Lord's name upon his lips must forsake wickedness.' " 2 Timothy 2:19. "All that dwell upon the earth shall worship him [the beast], whose names are not written in the book of life of the Lamb slain from the foundation of the world." Revelation 13:8, K.J.V.

God asks His people to walk so close to His purposes that the Holy Spirit can explode their talents into a great burst of witnessing and evangelism that will finish the spread of the gospel. The church cannot accomplish its task until the Holy Spirit takes control.

"It was by the confession and forsaking of sin, by earnest prayer and consecration of themselves to God, that the early disciples prepared for the outpouring of the Holy Spirit on the Day of Pentecost. The same work, only in greater degree, must be done now. Then the human agent had only to ask for the blessing, and wait for the Lord to perfect the work concerning him. . . . Only those who are living up to the light they have will receive greater light. Unless we are daily advancing in the exemplification of the active Christian virtues, we shall not recognize the manifestations of the Holy Spirit in the latter rain. It may be falling on hearts all around us, but we shall not discern or receive it."—*Testimonies to Ministers,* p. 507.

Trumpet blasts shattered the morning air day after day in the Israelite encampment—and later in the city of Jerusalem—as the Day of Atonement approached. "God, the Lord God, has spoken and summoned the world from the rising to the setting sun." Psalm 50:1. Today, God sounds the trumpet blasts of the signs of Christ's coming. Judgment is here. And He calls the earth to face it. Who will hear His voice?

"God shines out from Zion, perfect in beauty." Verse 2. When the Shekinah glory came to ancient Israel, Zion glowed with divine radiance. Where shines the Shekinah today? "When he shall appear, we shall be like him." 1 John 3:2, K.J.V.

"Our God is coming and will not keep silence: consuming fire runs before him and wreathes him closely round. He

74

summons heaven on high and earth to the judgement of his people." Psalm 50:3, 4.

Upon the effectiveness of the Spirit's activity will depend our inclusion in God's great command, "Gather to me my loyal servants, all who by sacrifice have made a covenant with me." Verse 5.

The Spirit is working now. Do you feel Him convicting you of sin, of the need for righteousness, of judgment to come? Have you felt His presence in your life guiding, directing? Has He multiplied your talents, given you gifts for God's glory? Are you preparing for the spiritual latter rain?

Right now, the Spirit waits to have more of you. He has many more things to communicate, more of God's will to explain, more of His power to impart.

CHAPTER 7

KEEPING CONTACT WITH GOD

"We have lost all contact with Flight No. . . ."

All too often the words spell disaster and heartache. Voices that a moment before spoke of angles and vectors, of approaches and landing time, suddenly go silent. Flight controllers frantically try to signal them. Airline officials brace themselves for tragedy.

Flying in New Guinea tests your nerves. Mountains soar upward in chain after chain. Updrafts and downdrafts fight for control of the aircraft.

Flight control authorities in New Guinea operate one of the most rigorous safety programs in the world. While over 250 airfields and landing strips flatten the tops of ridges or skirt highland valleys, only a handful boast control towers, and some do not even possess the smallest hut for passengers or visitors to wait in. Yet no plane takes off or lands without reporting its movements and flight plan. The island's Civil Aviation people know the location of every plane.

We waited for aircraft VH-SDA, with Colin Winch at the controls, to pick us up at Ambunti. The mission family stationed there had a powerful all-bands radio with which they could monitor aircraft flights. With the radio they would listen in as the small ships of the Adventist fleet talked to base. At set hours Ambunti would go on the air itself, talking to mission headquarters, or relaying messages.

Tension filled the missionary wife for a moment as she found the aircraft's frequency and waited. Her husband was flying with Colin. Then the pilot's clear voice, "Landing at Ambunti in ten minutes. Sierra Delta Alpha landing at Ambunti in ten minutes."

"Roger, Sierra Delta Alpha, report when on the ground at Ambunti." Immediately we began the frantic dash down the slippery clay path to the landing strip that runs at right angles from the Sepik River bank toward steep hills a mile or so away.

At first thought it seems impossible that God should keep contact with His millions of believers, know all about them, answer their prayers, even impress courses of action on their minds. Yet God does. Through prayer we reach for heaven and heaven reaches for us. Loss of contact with God wrecks even the stoutest faith in Him. Contact maintained steers us on a course toward heaven.

To pray is to let Jesus into our needs. To pray is to let God use His powers to help our distress. To pray lets God be glorified in our lives.

Promptings to Pray

"Here I stand knocking at the door; if anyone hears my voice and opens the door, I will come in and sit down to supper with him and he with me." Revelation 3:20.

God awaits our first trembling response to His request to enter our lives. Jesus stands outside the door of our hearts, knocking. His knocking prompts you to pray. Every true prayer originates from a divine impulse planted within. You cannot pray without God communicating with you through Christ and His Spirit. "The Spirit of truth . . . will glorify me, for everything that he makes known to you he will draw from what is mine. All that the Father has is mine, and that is why I said, 'Everything that he makes known to you he will draw from what is mine.'" John 16:13-15.

Think again for a moment of the triangle of prayer—you the one praying; God hearing; the object, person, or thing prayed about. Engineers regard the triangle as one of the strongest of all shapes. Prayer locks us and our needs in with God. A whole new set of relationships develops between God and man, and man with man, during prayer.

Prayer exposes our needs to the Sun of righteousness. "But unto you that fear my name shall the Sun of righteousness arise with healing in his wings." Malachi 4:2, K.J.V. God invites us to take the "Sun-cure." As the chilled, the aged, and the affluent flee from winter to find the sun, so the Christian flies to the Son that he might bask in the healing balm of heavenly "Sunshine." You have a place in the "Sun."

No pressure can break or distort the links that bind us and our needs to God. When we pray for our loved ones, they cannot escape the bonds that reach from us to them through God. They, too, feel the benefit of the warming rays of divine love. Prayer, like a magnifying glass, focuses God on them.

Prayer informs us of God's will. God does not need to know our problems. His omniscience compasses every one of them. But prayer opens our spiritual eyes to God's purposes. It moves us to begin working as Heaven's agents on earth. And prayer prevents us from thwarting, however unwittingly, God's plans.

You can see, then, how far from the reality of prayer the Pharisee's declaration was. He informed God of his own goodness, he used another's need to exalt his own righteousness, and he sought to manipulate God.

Prayer helps us define our needs. As we formulate them for presentation in prayer, we come to know what the real problem is. Often to define or figure out what a problem is, brings us a step closer toward an answer. Though we do not need to tell God of our needs, we may need to inform ourselves. How often we start out praying for something material, and then as we pray, we recognize that our real needs are spiritual. Prayer organizes a Christian's priorities, outlines his concerns, places life in perspective.

The School of Prayer

False religion seeks to objectify God—to turn him into an object. Pagan religions encase their gods in wood, stone, brass, and their priests manipulate the believers through physical control of the gods. Once God takes the form of an object, he ceases to be God. Prayer never seeks to manipulate God. The transcendent, omniscient Deity refuses to subject Himself to any man's connivings or even sincere propaganda. True prayer recognizes that God is the manipulator. We come in prayer to listen and learn.

Sketched on the wall of a dim recess in the temple of the Thousand Pillars in Madurai, India, I found a blueprint for a god. All the detail was there. Length of arms (either six or eight of them, I think), proportion of body, shape of head. A do-it-yourself god-kit. Naïve? Perhaps.

Demanding that God answer our prayers in a specific way of our own choosing structures God according to our wishes, not His plans. Certainly, telling God the alternative that we think suits best helps clarify issues for us. Yet our prayers must be according to God's will.

Daniel may well have feared the den of lions. But "God did not prevent Daniel's enemies from casting him into the lions' den; He permitted evil angels and wicked men thus far to accomplish their purpose; but it was that He might make the deliverance of His servant more marked, and the defeat of the enemies of truth and righteousness more complete. . . . A man whose heart is stayed upon God will be the same in the hour of his greatest trial as he is in prosperity, when the light and favor of God and of man beam upon him."—*Prophets and Kings,* pp. 543-545.

Prayer teaches much about God. He reveals Himself through prayer and its answers. How many homes experience sudden tragedies, crises of mind and spirit. Dread, sorrow, fear—all drive us closer and closer to God. Suddenly we find ourselves where we should have been all along. We have opened the door to our lives. Jesus is supping with us. The clouds hovering over us roll back. Peace pervades us. Although we learn much about God from such experiences, we might have known Him in the same way through prayer.

Prayer teaches us about ourselves. It gives and encourages

us to take time to contrast self with Christ. Prayer tells us how little our outward appearance reveals the sinful horror lurking within.

Prayer teaches about others. When we pray for others, it reinforces the Golden Rule in our attitudes toward them. Then we learn to sit where they sit, and in amazement we even see them as Christ might see them—wonderful prospects for the kingdom of God.

"The Lord turned the captivity of Job when he prayed, not only for himself, but for those who were opposing him. When he felt earnestly desirous that the souls that had trespassed against him might be helped, he himself received help. Let us pray, not only for ourselves, but for those who have hurt us, and are continuing to hurt us. Pray, pray, especially in your mind. Give not the Lord rest; for His ears are open to hear sincere, importunate prayers, when the soul is humbled before Him."—Ellen G. White in *S.D.A. Bible Commentary,* Vol. 3, p. 1141.

Whatever You Say, Lord

Are you an umbrella Christian? Too many people think that God's care should include absolute and complete protection from harm and danger. They would like to see Christians walking around unscathed while trouble and sorrow pelted like rain on the unbeliever.

You think that's exaggerating? Consider an incident in the life of Christ. "At that very time there were some people present who told him about the Galileans whose blood Pilate had mixed with their sacrifices. He [Christ] answered them: 'Do you imagine that, because these Galileans suffered this fate, they must have been greater sinners than anyone else in Galilee?' " Luke 13:1, 2.

The reverse of the coin puts a curse on all those who do not obey God. Thunderbolts of disaster hurl down on them.

The Bible supports neither position. Faith does bring rewards, but let us interpret faith's rewards correctly. Hope, joy, peace, security, purpose, forgiveness, cleansing, and victory are the miracles of faith. They are the umbrella that prayer does provide.

But we would not exclude the direct, recognizable answer to prayer. Answers happen. God answers prayers for the sick, prayers for conversion, prayers for safety, prayers for deliverance, prayers for financial help.

Think again about our prayer triangle. Remember that God recognizes our need. He knows about the wayward son and He is already working for him. He knows about the cancer eating out the life of a loved one. He knows about the vicious habit that continually seeks to devour our spiritual lives. He also knows the willful mind of man, the inexorable inroads of sin and disease, the weakness of human determination.

Then what does God do? How does He answer our prayers? If we but open the door and let Jesus come in, He will become part of our household: aware of our concerns; sharing the pain and heartache; joining us in spiritual battle. He will take control of our lives and problems.

God is answering your prayers now. He is strengthening your faith, showing you how to relate to sorrow and disappointment. Could you wish for better answers? Would you have God terrify the sinner to forced repentance, for example? Remember the love and sympathy of God and that He wants to save everyone He possibly can. "It is not that the Lord is slow in fulfilling his promise, as some suppose, but that he is very patient with you, because it is not his will for any to be lost, but for all to come to repentance." 2 Peter 3:9.

Jesus shares your concerns and works for eternal goals. His answers, His miracles lie in the context of eternal life.

God's Horn of Plenty

"Through nature and revelation, through His providence, and by the influence of His Spirit, God speaks to us. But these are not enough; we need also to pour out our hearts

81

to Him. In order to have spiritual life and energy, we must have actual intercourse with our heavenly Father. . . . In order to commune with God, we must have something to say to Him concerning our actual life."—Ellen G. White, *Steps to Christ,* p. 93.

Chief of all the blessings that prayer brings is forgiveness. The Jewish king Manasseh seduced thousands of his subjects to idolatry. Yet God heard his prayer and forgave him for his sinful deeds.

"Our heavenly Father waits to bestow upon us the fullness of His blessing. It is our privilege to drink largely at the fountain of boundless love. What a wonder it is that we pray so little! . . . The angels love to bow before God; they love to be near Him. They regard communion with God as their highest joy; and yet the children of earth, who need so much the help that God only can give, seem satisfied to walk without the light of His Spirit, the companionship of His presence."—*Ibid.,* p. 94.

Often we stop short of the blessing God seeks to give. Persevere in prayer. Continue steadfastly until the answer comes. "And he spake a parable unto them to the end that they ought always to pray, and not to faint." Luke 18:1, R.V. Business involvements and the tedious round of activity dissipate our desire to pray. We give up. Yet we should be like Paul said of Epaphras—that he was always striving in prayer for the people at Colossae. When we pray intensely for someone or some cause, we sympathize, we live with, we identify with that person or for that cause.

When sloth saps our desire to pray, we must go to the Spirit of prayer. He will renew our consciousness of need for more prayer and spiritual strength.

Opening the Channel

Our prime involvement in prayer is to search for God's will. "You do not get what you want, because you do not pray for it. Or, if you do, your requests are not granted because you pray from wrong motives, to spend what you get on your pleasures." James 4:2, 3.

"Our selfishness knows no bounds. In more or less naïve self-love we look upon everything with which we come in contact as existing for our sakes, as something for us to make use of and to utilize to our own advantage. . . .

"And we make no exception of God.

"As soon as we encounter Him, we immediately look upon Him as another means of gaining our own ends. . . . This is the reason why the natural man seldom finds that it pays to pray regularly to God. It requires too much effort, takes too much time, and is on the whole impracticable for the simple reason that one even forgets to pray."—O. Hallesby, *Prayer*, p. 95.

When such a person finds that God does not put Himself at his disposal in the way he thought He should, then that person becomes deeply offended and disappointed. When you cannot get what you ask for, why pray?

Yet even the spiritual man falls into such a trap. Remember the mother of James and John who asked Jesus that He might specially honor them in God's kingdom. In reply, Jesus, treating them with kindness and sympathy, explained God's will to them.

The Spirit of prayer commits Himself to reveal the will of God to us. "We do not even know how we ought to pray, but through our inarticulate groans the Spirit himself is pleading for us, . . . he pleads for God's people in God's own way." Romans 8:26, 27. Lovingly, kindly, He reminds us that just making requests is not the purpose of prayer. Too often our prayers for Christian enterprises and projects depend on the extent of our own involvement in them and a perhaps unexpressed desire for personal glory through their success.

"This is the confidence that we have in him, that, if we ask anything according to his will, he heareth us." 1 John 5:14, K.J.V. One of our greatest sins against God is that we do not talk to Him enough. Thus we do not uncover His will. Without practice no Christian will become a real man or woman of prayer. And practice asks perseverance.

How often prayer disappoints us because no sudden event occurs. We wonder if God hears us. Soon we begin speculating on what He wants *us* to do to answer the prayer. Yet He may not even want or seek our help. As at the wedding feast in Cana, our role is to listen and obey. Mary, Jesus' mother, expressed one of the great laws of prayer when she said, "Do whatever he tells you." John 2:5.

"As in this way we learn to know Jesus better and better, our prayers become quiet, confidential, and blessed conversations with Him, our best Friend, about the things that are on our minds, whether it be our own needs or the needs of others. We experience wonderful peace and security by leaving our difficulties, both great and small, with Him, who is not only solicitous for our welfare but who also understands what is best for us."—*Ibid.,* p. 37.

The Products of Prayer

My association with the Voice of Prophecy radio program in Australia began in 1956. As I faced the problems of finance and the frustrations of unfulfilled opportunities, I learned that the radio program, like so many other ventures of God, involves faith and prayer. Each Thursday morning we prayed for the needs of listeners and of the broadcast. In those days Australia was just facing the introduction of television, and the radio medium was making frantic switches in programming policy to meet the challenge—changes which affected the Voice of Prophecy. It was good to know that thousands of Christians joined us in prayer in our crises.

Prayer produces a united and powerful church. Prayer unites a family. Prayer heals breaches between friends. Prayer opens doors of service. Prayer puts us on God's side. And you could add endlessly to the list.

What a disaster, then, that the people of God pray so little!

"By the grace of Christ the apostles were made what they were. It was sincere devotion and humble, earnest prayer that brought them into close communion with Him. They sat together with Him in heavenly places. . . . By earnest, persevering prayer they obtained the endowment of the Holy Spirit, and then they went forth, weighted with the burden of saving souls, filled with zeal to extend the triumphs of the cross. . . .

"Shall we be less earnest than were the apostles? . . . Is not the Spirit of God to come today in answer to earnest, persevering prayer, and fill men with power? Is not God saying today to His praying, trusting, believing workers, who are opening the Scriptures to those ignorant of the precious truth they contain: 'Lo, I am with you alway, even unto the end of the world'? Matthew 28:20. Why, then, is the church so weak and spiritless?"—*Testimonies,* Vol. 7, p. 32.

Ellen G. White mentions many things for which we may rightly pray: for the salvation of youth and children, for clear perception to discern the Spirit's office and work, for daily bread both physical and spiritual, for enlightenment by the Spirit, for forgiveness, for the gift of the Spirit, for grace and strength, for guidance. She expands our vision of a prayer ministry to include other church members, the sick, the sorrowful. We may request transformation of character, for understanding of the times we live in, for wisdom. Perhaps even more importantly, she invites us to pray so that we shall know what to pray for.

"God does not say, Ask once, and you shall receive. He bids us ask. Unwearyingly persist in prayer. The persistent asking brings the petitioner into a more earnest attitude, and gives him an increased desire to receive the things for which he asks. . . .

"Our part is to pray and believe. Watch unto prayer. Watch, and co-operate with the prayer-hearing God."—Ellen G. White, *Christ's Object Lessons,* pp. 145, 146.

CHAPTER 8

WORDS – PRIME TOOL OF COMMUNICATORS

"The old Greeks had only theatres, occasional orators, and hard-to-come-by scrolls with which to compete. But today's would-be communicator contends with NBC, CBS, ABC, billboards, magazines, paperbacks, marquees, records of all sorts, and a zillion other distractions. Dead lies the Sunday evening church service, mortally wounded by radio and given the *coup de grâce* by Ed Sullivan. And pity the missionary whose mimeographed letter arrives in the same mail with the *Ladies Home Journal.*"–Sue Nichols, *Words on Target,* p. 9.

Ellen G. White wrote, "A little girl once asked me, 'Are you going to speak this afternoon?' 'No, not this afternoon,' I replied. 'I am very sorry,' she said. 'I thought you were going to speak, and I asked several of my companions to come. Will you please ask the minister to speak easy words that we can understand? Will you please tell him that we do not understand large words, like "justification" and "sanctification"? We do not know what these words mean.' "–*Counsels to Parents, Teachers, and Students,* p. 254.

How often teachers, parents, preachers, everyone, generally just fail to communicate! Babel appears not only in a confusion of tongues, but in words mouthed at each other that have no meaning to the recipient, or worse, convey a wrong meaning. Conveying Christ through the spoken or written word struggles not only with competition from the various media, but also competition from a secular culture, from hidden prejudices, and from unnamed fears.

"The Saviour's voice was as music to the ears of those who had been accustomed to the monotonous, spiritless preaching

86

of the scribes and Pharisees. He spoke slowly and impressively, emphasizing those words to which He wished His hearers to give special heed. Old and young, ignorant and learned, could catch the full meaning of His words."—*Ibid.*, p. 240.

"If . . . words are to enter men's hearts and bear fruit, they must be the right words shaped cunningly to pass men's defences and explode silently and effectually within their minds."—J. B. Phillips, quoted in *Words on Target*, p. 5.

The Right Words

A hotel desk clerk received a long distance call about an overnight reservation. "Do you want a room with a tub or a shower?" the clerk asked.

"What's the difference?" the caller replied.

"Well," came the patient response, "with a tub, you sit down."

That's how easily we go wrong in communicating. Somehow the clerk and the caller just didn't get together on the meaning of "difference." Not all lapses in communication are so amusing or so easily remedied.

To use words effectively lifts many of the roadblocks preventing communication. Often the person seeking to communicate is hindered by the fact that he has fuzzy ideas about what he intends to say, or speaks in haste or anger, or even really doesn't have anything to say. But employed properly, words can lift the spirit, persuade, convict, bring joy, and lead others to Christ.

Sir Winston Churchill rallied a gloomy, threatened Britain with words. "At that moment the only shield and the only weapons that democracy had against disaster were the words of Winston Churchill," Dorothy Thompson wrote. "The man with nothing but words—words gushing from the deepest springs of our glorious language—words of faith, fortitude, memory, hope, pride, humility, broke the frozen paralysis of a people and stood them on their feet, while the young anonymous eagles of the air beat off the threat to civilization."

Speaking of the use of words in speech Ellen G. White says, "Of all the gifts we have received from God, none is capable of being a greater blessing than this."—*Christ's Object Lessons,* p. 335. Whoever you are, wherever you are, as you use language to communicate with your son or daughter, husband or wife, neighbors, business associates, or government officials, you can vitally contribute to today's world and God's world of the future.

The magic of arranging words is one that captivates writers and public speakers. A simple adjustment in order, nuance, inflection, or tone changes the entire thrust of a phrase or sentence. In addition, words and phrases attach to themselves a history of meaning and tradition that often seems to bring a whole culture with them. For an American the phrase "Bill of Rights" summons a vision of a struggle for personal liberties stretching over two hundred years. For an Australian the word *Eureka!* conjures a vision of the common man resisting unjust oppression at the Eureka Stockade.

Think of the depth of spiritual insight that floods in with the words, "God so loved." Or the soaring hope that lifts us as we begin, "Let not your heart be troubled."

When Jesus "opened His lips to speak . . . every word was to some soul a savor of life unto life."—*Ibid.,* p. 338.

"We should speak of the mercy and loving-kindness of God, of the matchless depths of the Saviour's love. Our words should be words of praise and thanksgiving. If the mind and heart are full of the love of God, this will be revealed in the conversation. . . . Great thoughts, noble aspirations, clear perceptions of truth, unselfish purposes, yearnings for piety and holiness, will bear fruit in words that reveal the character of the heart treasure."—*Ibid.*

Lying Lips

Jesus proclaimed, "I am . . . the truth." His words of truth inflamed those threatened by their concepts. Christ stated, "He who sent me speaks the truth, and what I heard from

88

him I report to the world." John 8:26. As Christ continued His unfolding of the relationship between Father and Son, the Pharisees' skepticism toward Him increased. Finally Christ identified their problem: unbelief in Christ's mission which grows under the influence of the first liar.

Satan's words are made of whole cloth—a veritable fabric of lies. Satan's first lie concerned the nature of his own self. The thought of remaining a merely created being riled him. As a result he developed a false self-image and began to make claims for that false self. Thus he became the father of lies.

Adam and Eve stepped into the same trap. Having lost heaven through perpetrating a lie about himself, and thus about the God who created him, Satan snickered a seductive thought to Eve. And Eve fell to the lure of a false image of herself—a created being achieving the powers and insights of God.

By denying reality, we side with Satan. All forms of false communication take that risk. Novels, dramatic theater, and fictional films transport us from reality into a world of falsity. Here Satan flourishes.

When we lie, we deny the truth about ourselves, the truth about others, and the truth about God's world. What situations justify lying? According to Ellen G. White we are never to tell a lie by word or example. See *My Life Today,* p. 331. "No lie is of the truth. If we follow cunningly devised fables, we unite with the enemy's forces against God and Christ."—*Selected Messages,* Book One, p. 194. Only a life of complete faith and harmony with Christ can present the truth in every situation.

One of the more insidious temptations of modern society is to turn people into objects or things. Call a man "commie," "jew-boy," or "nigger" and he becomes less than human. We can then take specific instances of misdeeds conducted by individuals and apply them to the whole group. In doing so, we create a lie about ourselves—we claim superiority over others, and the Bible denies that any group of people is inherently better than another. We tell a lie about God, who made all of us. When we see how a lie can hurt others and spoil the image of the true God within us, we should weep.

As Christians awake to the tumult of the last days, they should remember the concept of "the big lie." Speaking of the work of satanic antichrist, Paul says, "It will be attended by all the powerful signs and miracles of the Lie, and all the deception that sinfulness can impose on those doomed to destruction." 2 Thessalonians 2:9, 10.

Those Wonderful Words

If Satan is Lie, Christ is Truth.

When we speak the truth in the principle of love, we speak as God speaks. Actually we are letting Christ speak through us.

Today we find ourselves buried in words. Once the gossip of neighbor, the chitchat of friends, the news of the town crier, the conversation of the family circled the individual. Now strangers shout at us from the television tube. Politicians wheedle our support by newspaper, direct-mail advertisements, and every other way available to transmit words. Madison Avenue strings words of magic to seduce our pocketbooks.

I have a friend who has a hearing aid for both ears. He tells of the time when he decided that he should buy his first hearing aid. Suddenly his world reeled under a cacophony of sounds. Doors closing, his own breathing, birds chirping, people chatting, the whir of the air conditioner—all produced acute discomfort. Through years of poor hearing he had lost the ability to filter out unneeded sounds. For a month he went through agony until he again learned to ignore unwanted noise. A few years later he decided he needed hearing in stereo and bought a second aid. Once more he suffered, just as acutely as the first time.

If we are to hear the word of God amid the torrents of words flowing over us, we need spiritual filters. The words of life are there all right, but we have to tune ourselves to hear them, read them, use them.

Malachi records a series of complaints against Israel. God chided them for failing to understand spiritual truth. "You have wearied the Lord with your talk. You ask, 'How have we wearied him?' By saying that all evildoers are good in the eyes of the Lord, that he is pleased with them, or by asking, 'Where is the God of justice?' " Malachi 2:17.

Again he writes, "You have used hard words about me, says the Lord, and then you ask, 'How have we spoken against thee?' You have said, 'It is useless to serve God; what do we gain from the Lord of Hosts by observing his rules?' " Malachi 3:13, 14.

The cure? They needed to sit down and pay attention to God and begin thanking Him for what He had done.

"Then those who feared the Lord talked together, and the Lord paid heed and listened. A record was written before him of those who feared him and kept his name in mind. They shall be mine, says the Lord of Hosts." Verses 16, 17.

"The time has come for men to stop what they are doing and praise the Lord.

"Praise him in the command ships soaring through outer space. Praise him in the bowels of the earth, in the mine pits of the Ruhr and Wales and the Ural Mountains. . . .

"Let the name of the Lord be magnified upon the computer, the electric typewriter, the cassette, the transistor. Let him be glorified on back-to-back multiplex FM stereo. Let God be praised on full-color network television at prime evening time."—*Decision*, May, 1971, p. 2.

Indeed, praise Him in the home. Praise Him to your neighbors and your business associates. Praise Him for His goodness, His love, His Christ. Let us fill the earth with His praises.

A Choice of Words

"As he thinketh in his heart, so is he." Proverbs 23:7, K.J.V.
"When the soul has been cleansed, it is the duty of the

91

Christian to keep it undefiled. Many seem to think that the religion of Christ does not call for the abandonment of daily sins, the breaking loose from habits which have held the soul in bondage. . . . They do not show a thoughtful care in the choice of words. Too often, fretful, impatient words are spoken, words which stir the worst passions of the human heart. Such ones need the abiding presence of Christ in the soul."—Ellen G. White in *S.D.A. Bible Commentary*, Vol. 3, p. 1157.

The Apostle James' chapter on communication emphasizes the importance of how we use words. He equates a careless tongue with a serpent spitting venom. Words have tremendous power for both evil and good. They can change the world. All communication seeks to produce change—change in knowledge, change in feelings, change in attitudes. The question is, How are we transforming the world with our words? How are we altering ourselves? The gossip shifts a person's character at will. The liar turns truth into falsehood. On the other hand, the peacemaker changes strife to serenity. The Holy Spirit uses the human witness to help convert sinners.

You think your words have no effect? "Every act of love, every word of kindness, every prayer in behalf of the suffering and oppressed, is reported before the eternal throne and placed on heaven's imperishable record."—*Testimonies*, Vol. 5, p. 133.

Our words reveal ourselves. A tree bears again the seed that gave it life. Yet our words not only show our hidden natures, they also help change those natures. When we speak words of cheer, we help ourselves rise over discouragement. We brighten our own days by accentuating the positive. And confessing Christ, we help confirm our changed nature.

Our words encourage others. One time a child perched dangerously in the window of a burning building. A fireman rode on the end of the ladder raised near her. He reached for the little girl, but the smoke drove him back. Suddenly a voice in the crowd yelled, "Cheer him!" A shout of encouragement went up. In a moment the fireman had the trapped child safe in his arms.

Many succumb to temptation, sink from discouragement, because no one cheers them on. Never hesitate to say an encouraging word. Many people live in the shadowy areas of life. Beam the sunshine of your cheer upon them.

Guides leading mountaineers in snowy regions caution about avalanches. Even a spoken word may start a deadly slide. In a similar manner, think before you speak words of discouragement to anyone. Some hearts linger so close to despair that one dispiriting word can send them hurtling downward.

"Do not tell your troubles to your fellow mortals, but carry everything to God in prayer. Make it a rule never to utter one word of doubt or discouragement. You can do much to brighten the life of others and strengthen their efforts, by words of hope and holy cheer."—*Steps to Christ*, pp. 119, 120.

How can we choose the right words to say?

"Angels are watching with intense interest to see how man is dealing with his fellow men. When they see one manifest Christlike sympathy for the erring, they press to his side and bring to his remembrance words to speak that will be as the bread of life to the soul. . . . Before communicating with men, commune with Christ. . . . Let your heart break for the longing it has for God, for the living God. . . . Then ask and receive. . . . Let the glorious conceptions of God possess your mind. . . . The Holy Spirit will take the things of God and show them unto you, conveying them as a living power into the obedient heart."—*Christ's Object Lessons*, p. 149.

Defining the Good

I serve on a number of committees that decide what words the church will use in speaking to the world and its own members. As an author I know the care with which editors peruse every word one writes. Frequently I have had to edit material myself. Even a lifetime will not produce one page

93

of perfect copy, a perfect sonnet, or a perfect broadcast. We may think them perfect, but someone can always point out where we could improve them, polish them up.

Yet, for all their imperfections, the church has used the media mightily. A few years ago an Anglican minister discussed with me the pioneering work of the Adventist Church in Bible correspondence courses. "That was an idea right from the heart of God," he commented. Agreed. So much of what we do succeeds not because of ourselves, our talents, our skills, but because the Lord is with it.

As we move toward the final events of our present world, our communications efforts must radiate the penetrating power of the Word of God and the Holy Spirit. It is not enough just to say something to the world, we must say the right thing for our time—that God is redeeming the world in and through Jesus Christ. Our church's message finds its genius, its source, in angelic proclamations in the Book of Revelation. No Christian communicator is worth anything without the Word of God. No Adventist communicator is worth anything without the special message God has given him.

You must approach the world sensibly, intelligently. An overall look at what you are doing to reach it may reveal many weaknesses in your attempts to communicate. And don't just think of the printed material you are distributing, or the broadcasts you are airing. Think of the way your church looks, the way your people dress, the community involvement of the church. What your church does will communicate, will tell something to its observer whether you wish it or not.

"I have been shown that the disciples of Christ are His representatives upon the earth; and God designs that they shall be lights in the moral darkness of this world, dotted all over the country, in the towns, villages, and cities, 'a spectacle unto the world, and to angels, and to men.' If they obey the teachings of Christ in His Sermon on the Mount, they will be seeking continually for perfection of Christian character, and will be truly the light of the world, channels

94

through which God will communicate His divine will, the truth of heavenly origin, to those who sit in darkness and who have no knowledge of the way of life and salvation."—*Testimonies,* Vol. 2, p. 631.

Speaking Christ's Word

"Marshall McLuhan, the stimulating commentator on the effect of communication media, insists that in the age of television it is not written but oral communication that is once more becoming the channel of interaction that binds our lives, that determines our destinies.

"In these interactions we achieve and we gain satisfaction—if we are prepared for them. Being prepared for communication does not necessarily mean knowing what we will say or hear. It means knowing what we are trying to accomplish and providing ourselves with the necessary perceptions—perceptions of the situation, of the subject matter and, probably most of all, perceptions of the other person, whether speaker or listener."—R. T. Oliver, H. P. Zelko, P. D. Holtzman, *Communicative Speaking and Listening,* pp. 5, 6.

At least some of the modern students of the communications media refer to today as the postliterate age. Information comes through audio-visual devices rather than books. Some even suggest that we would serve illiterates better by teaching them to interpret audio-visual messages than by insisting that they concentrate on learning to read. In the age of "Sesame Street" and the high school graduate that has just completed 17,000 hours of television viewing, the church may well ponder the alternatives it faces. The church has more channels to use in reaching people than just the printed and traditional spoken word.

Paul faced an articulate and well-informed society when he went to Corinth. His solution? He communicated by preaching Christ—not philosophy or theory. While some called his words folly, he overlooked their rebuke and continued preaching the person of Christ. In the end his emphasis on

Christ-centered words reached through their shield of sophistication.

Highly structured reasoning, proof texts, and the like continue to have their importance, but such approaches as confrontation evangelism, New Testament Witnessing, and emphasis on the "Four Spiritual Laws" are producing even greater results. What should that teach us? That God's church can best reach others when it speaks of its own experience with Christ. Anybody is most convincing when he is telling others what has actually happened to him.

Psychology, science, archaeology, counseling, homiletics, have their share in achieving success in communicating to others, but the nitty-gritty of the effective use of words lies in the message we bring and our involvement with it. People want to know how we see Jesus, what we know and feel about Him. How He has revealed Himself to us. How they can experience Him. They see the Bible as a road to an experience with God rather than an amazing collection of truths that someone may tabulate and arrange in different ways to produce doctrines. And in this they come back to the essence of the Bible—a revelation of a personal God whom we can experience. The Greeks arrived at God by logic, the Jews by revelation and experience.

In this context it is no surprise that the call of the last days is to a God who reveals Himself. And what may we communicate to our changing world? The Christ we see and know from personal experience and from revelation.

CHAPTER 9

FALSE SIGNALS – CROSSED LINES

The experience lives with me as one of my more embarrassing moments. A fellow minister and I were talking on the phone. After a few minutes we began to discuss another minister whom we thought had some problems with denominational policy. We became quite frank about our mutual acquaintance, agreeing that he surely needed help.

I forgot the conversation until a few days later when I happened to be with the very man I had discussed. His coolness toward me alarmed me. I asked what was the problem. As he told me, I wanted to shrivel away. In a freak occurrence, for it took place in a large city, he had dialed me that day. The telephone lines became crossed, and he had heard our dissection of him. Every word of it!

Fortunately he forgave me, and I'm glad the experience came when I was still quite new in the ministry. It taught me many lessons. One, that crossed lines rarely work to anyone's advantage.

When we were beginning the Adventist World Radio broadcasts in Europe late in 1971, our transmissions had a lot of trouble with competing stations. Shortwave broadcasting resembles a free-for-all. Rules on radio frequencies do exist but are often honored in the breach. An empty space on the radio dial attracts smaller stations like a rocket homing on target.

AWR's 250,000-watt voice soon made it evident that competition for its particular frequency would have to cease. Within weeks our clear signals penetrated most areas. Eventually even an Eastern European station chose other frequencies to broadcast on, and our programs produced a heartening response from inside the socialist republics.

Just as technical facilities may foul easily, so the Christian's communications can suffer a host of barriers and interferences. Communications that start clearly from God's word may attract so much static that they fail completely. Or the channel of communication may produce its own interference, its own blockage.

Doctors describe atherosclerosis as a process whereby the arteries accumulate fatty deposits so that the blood finds it increasingly difficult to reach its destination. One great problem of the church today lies in its members and leaders—when we refuse to let the message flow freely and fully through us, we hinder God's communicative ministry.

Sin rears the ultimate barrier between God and man, and between man and man. It inflates the ego and denies any need for God. Sin manipulates people, is self-centered, and produces confusion.

Communication Without God

"In certain situations people talk and listen easily, their minds stimulated by enthusiasm for an idea or by the company they are in. In other situations they feel reticent, withdrawn, and hesitant to enter into communicative give-and-take. Situations, purposes, topics, and people are all part of the explanation for these differences. A basic problem in personal effectiveness is learning how to recognize and adapt to bonds and barriers that facilitate and inhibit communication. Bonds between people invite transaction. Barriers insulate people from one another. Both as speakers and as listeners people need to learn how to capitalize on bonds and how to convert barriers into bonds."—*Communicative Speaking and Listening,* p. 17.

Jesus showed the greatest mastery in converting barriers into bonds. Seeking water from a well near Samaria, He completely demolished the barrier between Samaritan and Jew and built a bond with eternal life in the heart of the woman He met. Thomas could not take the leap of faith and believe in the resurrected Christ. But Jesus turned the doubter into one of His great apostles.

"In the Teacher sent from God, heaven gave to men its best and greatest. He who had stood in the councils of the Most High, who had dwelt in the innermost sanctuary of the Eternal, was the One chosen to reveal in person to humanity the knowledge of God."—*Education*, p. 73.

Christ entered a world where the knowledge of God was vanishing. "As they ceased to recognize the Divine, they ceased to regard the human. Truth, honor, integrity, confidence, compassion, were departing from the earth. Relentless greed and absorbing ambition gave birth to universal distrust. The idea of duty, of the obligation of strength to weakness, of human dignity and human rights, was cast aside as a dream or a fable."—*Ibid.*, p. 75.

Judging God by themselves and the actions of others, men circulated false ideas about Him. Christian communication still faces similar problems. Like Christ, we must approach the barriers the world raises with love—His love. We demonstrate such love through lives that reflect God's will.

Besides love, Christ came with sympathy and faith. "Looking upon them with hope, He inspired hope. Meeting them with confidence, He inspired trust. Revealing in Himself man's true ideal, He awakened, for its attainment, both faith and desire."—*Ibid.*, p. 80.

Building Babel Anew

Men once built a literal tower of Babel. Today's Babel builders might well be the scientists, technologists, philosophers, theologians, and statesmen who dismiss God and exalt man, his mind, his ideas. Up in their ivory towers they twitter with excitement about the newest miracle of the race's inventive genius. But do they really say anything more than a string of words? I do not intend to be antiknowledge or anti-intellectual, yet to build a tower of knowledge, science, and technology without God is to construct a twentieth-century Babel.

And Christians, even the churches, may have their own Babels. We build a Babel when we think ourselves superior, when we work without thought of God, when we laud men for the works of God. The result? Confusion, crossed lines, and blocked channels.

No one hears the voice of Christ when ego shouts for attention. Believability vanishes. Sincerity dies. People do not perceive that you are interested in them. A recent report of the U.S. Navy indicated that the old command "Now hear this! Now hear this!" had lost some of its effectiveness. Why? Because dull, lifeless voices conveyed the impression that they were not interested in the people they wanted to reach.

Christ worked effectively because He transmitted a feeling that He was one of us. One important communicative process is to build or find a common ground. A little girl in a Pennsylvania school walked up to a little boy and said, "I've been to the San Diego zoo. Where have you been?"

The surprised youngster said, "I've been to the San Diego zoo, too." Just that much common ground, but they became firm friends.

Evangelists know that they are much more effective when they start with their audience on something familiar to them. Only then can any kind of interaction begin to take place. "In a given instance speaker and listener may build a barrier or they may build a bond. . . . Interaction will depend upon reduction of the insulating barrier. If one or both seek their shared associations and experiences, 'one-of-us-ness' can be found and the barrier converted into a bond."—*Communicative Speaking and Listening,* p. 19.

"To the weak I became weak, to win the weak," Paul said. "Indeed, I have become everything in turn to men of every sort, so that in one way or another I may save some. All this I do for the sake of the Gospel, to bear my part in proclaiming it." 1 Corinthians 9:22, 23.

Today Babel doesn't exist only in the thousands of languages around the globe, but also in our hearts. Babel is dispersion from God.

How may we draw the world together at the feet of the Redeemer? By destroying the pride of Babel. By joining Christ with our lives so that we might successfully identify with a world of needy men and women.

The Big Lie

Hitler boasted in the success of "the big lie." Goebbels, his propaganda chief, worked on the theory that if you make a lie big enough, most people will believe it.

A lie stalks the truth of God in our day. As never before it barricades minds against truth. The lie takes many forms, but all of them center around a denial of God.

Satan began the big lie when he rejected God's claim and rulership over him. Today other forms of the big lie, the denial of God, fill the world. No matter how erudite, how sophisticated, how rational they may seem, to deny God is to lie. Evolution denies God. Humanism denies God. Materialism denies God. Build your own list—you'll need a stack of writing pads.

Ever since the first sin in heaven, the evil one has built toward our day, fabricating a structure of lies that will block mankind from hearing the voice of God. In Eden the lie took the form of a false picture of the nature of God and of false hopes for man. God, in the Old Testament, defined it as idolatry, false worship. Christ, in the New Testament, saw it as hypocrisy, false reflections of God walking the streets of Jerusalem in the persons of the Pharisees. Daniel predicted its manifestation in religion using the power of the state for its purposes.

Where does the lie surface today?

Daniel says, "It aspired to be as great as the Prince of the host, suppressed his regular offering and even threw down his sanctuary. The heavenly hosts were delivered up, and it raised itself impiously against the regular offering and threw true religion to the ground." Daniel 8:11, 12.

Jesus predicted, "Impostors will come claiming to be messiahs or prophets, and they will produce great signs and wonders to mislead even God's chosen, if such a thing were possible." Matthew 24:24.

Peter had his report from the future, "In the last days there will come men who scoff at religion and live self-indulgent lives, and they will say: 'Where now is the promise of his coming?' " 2 Peter 3:3, 4.

John "saw another beast, which came up out of the earth; it had two horns like a lamb's, but spoke like a dragon. It wielded all the authority of the first beast. . . . It worked great miracles, even making fire come down from heaven to earth before men's eyes." Revelation 13:11-13.

Thus Satan builds the big lie and communicates error as truth with the result that millions upon millions accept spiritual disaster.

The remedy? First a proclamation, "Fear God, and give glory to him; for the hour of his judgment is come: and worship him that made heaven and earth." Revelation 14:7, K.J.V.

Next a warning, "Babylon is fallen, is fallen. . . . If any man worship the beast, . . . the same shall drink of the wine of the wrath of God." Verses 8-10, K.J.V.

Finally, a source of truth. "Here is the patience of the saints: here are they that keep the commandments of God, and the faith of Jesus." Verse 12, K.J.V.

The medium that God uses for proclamation, for warning, for presenting truth? God's people.

Problems With the Receiver

How can we make truth root deeply into the life? Jesus sought to illustrate how through the parable of the good seed. In a way the parable is more a definition of the problems of communicating the gospel than a condemnation of those in whom the seed of the gospel comes to rest.

Some lives are indeed stony. Social, educational, environmental, and personal situations make them so. Should we turn away from them? No, we must break the stone down, bring soil to the rough places, water and nurture the seed. Frequently the Holy Spirit softens hearts through our care and love.

Some lives choke with weeds of doubt, discouragement, and anxiety. Our role should be that of cultivators of the soil. We must seek ways of removing the weeds that shade the plant from light and rob it of food. Welfare work, inner city programs, providing food for the poor, teaching deprived children, and laboring for the underprivileged can cultivate men's hearts.

People often create an environment that wilts the gospel. Often we need to help improve the environment before God's word can produce a harvest. Generations of Adventist missionaries have carried a special brand of social help to lands where disease, poverty, ignorance, and superstition hold control. Perhaps some of the more affluent lands need similar concerns for the environment that inhibits the communication of truth.

Communication must match the group to whom we direct it. The Voice of Prophecy's "Wayout" program contacts hundreds of thousands of youth—not just hippies, but almost all regular young people who want something to meet their needs. Similar material for other special groups might meet with like results. "Soul Food" tracts have enjoyed huge success in black ghettos. The church may learn a lesson from the success of special interest radio stations and magazines. They attract and hold an audience because they speak the particular language of a group of people. The church still has many segments of the public that it has not yet touched. For example, where are the church's special ministries for the rich, the intellectual?

History records many examples of genocide. The church may also be guilty of spiritual genocide if its members dismiss *any* race, group of people, class, or status as unworthy of

103

attention or too difficult to reach.

"The good seed may for a time lie unnoticed in a cold, selfish, worldly heart, giving no evidence that it has taken root; but afterward, as the Spirit of God breathes on the soul, the hidden seed springs up, and at last bears fruit to the glory of God. In our lifework we know not which shall prosper, this or that. This is not a question for us to settle. We are to do our work, and leave the results with God."—*Christ's Object Lessons*, p. 65.

Perhaps, too, in our planning of the work of God we should remember that not all wisdom and understanding reside with the rich and powerful. The church needs to involve more people—youth, practical working men, women, the poor, the deprived, as well as the rich and educated in its strategy.

Blanking the Source

A few years ago the Faith for Today television program had Dr. Albert Shepard, the famed expert on human motivation, conduct a survey on reasons why people accepted the invitation to study Bible correspondence lessons and what they expected from them. The survey highlighted some of the problems of communicating the gospel.

Great anticipation accompanied the request for the lessons. In combining our society's most powerful communications medium with the ancient wisdom of the world's most famous book, Faith for Today conjured in the minds of viewers images of hope and solutions to problems. One woman called the lessons "an envelope full of faith."

Yet there were problems. Clearly the lessons pleased many people, but a few looked for more personal help than the lessons provided. They had personal problems beyond the scope of any Bible lesson. Loneliness and deprivation of various kinds motivated many to write. Frustrated with the kinds of lives they led, they grasped at the lessons as an escape from unhappy reality. Such problems can obscure God's real message.

104

Other things block our understanding of God. Consider our concepts of God Himself.

The gods of the nations around ancient Israel filled the role the flag has in the United States. They rallied the people to patriotic fervor, armed their spirits for battle, soared or fell in power with the people who worshiped them. Nations played spiritual one-upmanship with each other. Like the little child who boasts, "My daddy is bigger than your daddy," Israel wanted to play such a game with Jehovah. When God wouldn't respond to their whims, they turned to an idol, thinking it might cater to their fanciful notions. Their lives and actions distorted their knowledge of the true God.

Yet we can do similar things. We put on filters that screen out God and let the inducements of the world reach us. Mental blocks against religion force God out of the thinking of many. After the incident at Kadesh God had to wait for a new generation before He could find people without mental blocks to the conquest of Canaan. How much do we believe that God can do what He says?

"Had Adventists, after the great disappointment in 1844, held fast their faith, and followed on unitedly in the opening providence of God, receiving the message of the third angel and in the power of the Holy Spirit proclaiming it to the world, they would have seen the salvation of God, the Lord would have wrought mightily with their efforts, the work would have been completed, and Christ would have come ere this to receive His people to their reward."—*Selected Messages,* Book One, p. 68.

Don't blame our spiritual ancestors. Look inside to see if we are also blanking out God's plans.

Frequently we do not study enough, prepare enough, agonize enough, grow enough. "We have much to say, much that is difficult to explain, now that you have grown so dull of hearing. For indeed, though by this time you ought to be teachers, you need someone to teach you the ABC of God's oracles over again; it has come to this, that you need milk instead of solid food. Anyone who lives on milk, being an infant, does not know what is right. But grown men can take solid food; their perceptions are trained by long use to discriminate between good and evil." Hebrews 5:11-14.

How Love Penetrates

Christ won back the world on the cross. God owns it though evil lingers in power a little longer. Still He has the power to roll over the Maginot Line of sin, bypass its fortifications, and take over any life.

But He uses a strange weapon—love. This chief weapon of Heaven's arsenal, manifested in the death of Jesus Christ, destroys squadrons of "old men" of sin. No concrete bunker of sin, indifference, or fear is proof against the explosive power of divine love.

And the church can have love on its side.

Love was working in us when we first responded to Jesus. "He first loved us." Love surrounds every person on earth. Christ's sacrifice empowers that love to redeem. That is why we may picture Christ eternally standing at the door of the heart, knocking to enter. He waits outside every door that has not opened to Him. And He sups with everyone who has asked Him in.

"The love of God embraces all mankind. . . . Christ intended that a greater work should be done in behalf of men than we have yet seen. He did not intend that such large numbers should choose to stand under the banner of Satan and be enrolled as rebels against the government of God. The world's Redeemer did not design that His purchased inheritance should live and die in their sins. Why, then, are so few reached and saved? It is because so many of those who profess to be Christians are working in the same lines as the great apostate. Thousands who know not God might today be rejoicing in His love if those who claim to serve Him would work as Christ worked."—*Testimonies*, Vol. 6, p. 273.

Love conquers. Here is power that overcomes our communications problems. It penetrates the barriers sin raises.

With love the inarticulate speak of God's care. With love the shy, the nervous, may do more than the most eloquent speaker. Love transcends human weaknesses and inadequacies. With poor words but great love we may yet serve our God.

CHAPTER 10

THREE-WAY TRANSMITTER COMPLEX

Twice a day the family of small mission ships that ply the South Seas link themselves by radio with Adventist headquarters. Each takes turn in receiving and sending messages. Twenty-three ships in all, they range from sedate river launches to genuine ocean-going small ships that can weather the tropical storms driving across the straits and waterways of the island groups.

The mission headquarters radio shack buzzes with activity as the sked—the time of radio contact—approaches. Transmitter and receiver warm up. The radio operator seeks the correct frequency. Then the operator, usually a missionary wife whose husband is probably on one of those ships, begins to call in the family. Also on the sked, remote mission stations wait their turn.

MV *Ka Seli* reports, "Am anchored at Silovuti. Expect big crowd at meetings tonight. Did you get the parts for our washer?"

The *Dani* queries, "Could you give me the time for the arrival of that General Conference man?"

A little more excitement grips the listeners as the *Light* reports, "One of our nurses at Hatzfeldhaven needs medical care. Am flying her out to Madang. Appreciate your prayers."

Each hears what the other is saying, and a bond of oneness and unity grows between the mission families and their national associates. Their transmitters and receivers keep them together.

And it is that way with the individual family. No, we don't warm up radio sets and tune wave bands. But the family consists of a continuous communicating complex, both within its own structure of family members and as a unit to the world and community. The ways the various members of the family respond to each other shape not only the nature of the family, but also the personality of each family member. For the Christian family such communication must be three-way. Thus the world transmits to the family and the family to the world. The family talks and communicates within itself. And the family speaks to God and listens for Him.

What does the home provide its participants? Food, shelter, and other material necessities. But more than that, it offers training, discipline, and personality improvement. And that's not all. Mutual concern, love, a sense of joint destiny, create an invaluable sense of togetherness.

Yet today the home fractures as an institution under a multisided attack. How valid is the home in the day of premarital freedoms, the pill, the technological society, the commune, and shifting ethical mores?

"The garden of Eden was a representation of what God desired the whole earth to become. . . . Thus in course of time the whole earth might be occupied with homes and schools where the words and the works of God should be studied, and where the students should thus be fitted more and more fully to reflect, throughout endless ages, the light of the knowledge of His glory."—*Education,* p. 22.

The Family in Crisis

"The family has been called the 'giant shock absorber' of society—the place to which the bruised and battered individual returns after doing battle with the world, the one stable point in an increasingly flux-filled environment. As the super-industrial revolution unfolds, this 'shock absorber' will come in for some shocks of its own.

"Social critics have a field day speculating about the family. The family is 'near the point of complete extinction,' says Ferdinand Lundberg, author of *The Coming World Transformation.* 'The family is dead except for the first year or two of child raising,' according to psychoanalyst William Wolf. 'This will be its only function.' "—Alvin Toffler, *Future Shock,* p. 238.

Sociologists talk of the impact of the new technology which programs birth, and may even remove it from the mother's womb; of professional parents; of communal families; of temporary marriage. As we hurtle into tomorrow at ever-accelerating rates of change, family life will find itself subject to fierce forces.

Seventh-day Adventist Christians may wonder if the Lord will actually permit outside forces to distort marriage so. Yet if Noah's day fully repeats itself and Sodom rebuilds itself, then our homes face undreamed-of crises.

Problems abound and grow more frightening. "We can orbit the earth, bring back samples of the moon, yet somehow we have not been able to devise a way for a man and a woman to live together with a guarantee of harmony and personal growth. . . . The bookstores are bulging with all kinds of advice from how to fight fairly in love and marriage to what the facets of a sensuous person are. . . . The divorce rate mounts monthly. Children of unhappy and broken homes, too often ill equipped to relate to or understand their own feelings, perpetuate the struggle; and internalized anxiety and guilt have, if anything, increased."—William C. Loveless, "The Vanishing American Family," *Gleaner,* February 7, 1972, pp. 5, 6.

What would God speak to the family today? Does He know of the threats facing it? Can He provide continuity for the love relationship He inaugurated in Eden?

"The husband must give his wife the same sort of love that Christ gave to the Church, when he sacrificed himself for her." "The love a man gives his wife is the extending of his love for himself to enfold her." "In practice what I have said amounts to this: let every one of you who is a husband love his wife as he loves himself, and let the wife reverence her husband." Ephesians 5:25, 28, 33, Phillips.

But just a moment. Don't get the wrong picture.

110

"Love" for Paul does not equate with any normal interpretation we give the word. Paul means "love-as-a-principle," not the love described in *The Sensuous Woman* and similar books. Nor is it love that adulates blindly, nor even the warm glow that surrounds a successful interpersonal relationship. Only love-as-a-principle will save the home and your family.

The Bible describes love-as-a-principle as "Love never faileth." That's quite a promise!

Speaking Love

Love (remember we mean by the term, love-as-a-principle) seeks always to communicate intelligently, for the best good of the parties involved, and with God in mind.

A contemporary wall poster gives the following advice:

CHILDREN LEARN WHAT THEY LIVE

If a child lives with criticism
    he learns to condemn.
If a child lives with hostility
    he learns to fight.
If a child lives with ridicule
    he learns to be shy.
If a child lives with shame
    he learns to feel guilty.
If a child lives with tolerance
    he learns to be patient.
If a child lives with encouragement
    he learns confidence.
If a child lives with praise
    he learns to appreciate.
If a child lives with fairness
    he learns justice.
If a child lives with security
    he learns to have faith.

If a child lives with approval
he learns to like himself.
If a child lives with acceptance and fairness
he learns to find love in the world.

"A house with love in it, where love is expressed in words and looks and deeds, is a place where angels love to manifest their presence, and hallow the scene by rays of light from glory."—*Testimonies*, Vol. 2, p. 417.

The home provides more frequent contact and interaction between small numbers of persons than any other unit of society. For that reason parents and marriage partners risk injuring their relationships if they do not approach family communication intelligently and prayerfully. I do not know if anyone has ever tried estimating the number of communication interactions between a parent and child before the child leaves home, or between husband and wife over a lifetime, but it must run to millions. And communication in the home produces change, educates, determines the future, solidifies relationships or cracks them.

Recent experiments with premature babies and other infants that must stay in the hospital for long periods show the importance of communication at the earliest ages. Babies held and cuddled grew faster and fatter than those handled mechanically and minimally.

As a child learns to understand words, and even before through the tone of voice, speech communication begins to mold and shape his future. You can't start applying love to your speech too soon.

"Satan and his host are making the most powerful efforts to sway the minds of the children, and they must be treated with candor, Christian tenderness, and love. This will give you a strong influence over them, and they will feel that they can repose unlimited confidence in you. Throw around your children the charms of home and of your society."—*Ibid.*, Vol. 1, pp. 387, 388.

And what applies to parent-child relationships applies with

equal force to husband and wife. An input of mutual love and respect programs a successful future. How often we hurt with words. Yet how easily words can heal.

Farmer Mackay had come to the sunset years. His wife and he had lived together as models of harmony and happiness for more than sixty years. Their children reflected the security and godliness of the home.

"Why have you been so happy? What is your secret?" people would ask.

Each inquirer received the same treatment. Mackay would dig deep in his pocket and produce a large pocket watch. "Read what's on it," he would say. "Sarah's father gave it to me the day we were married."

And the person would find inscribed on its dial the words, "Say something nice to Sarah, today." Each day he had seen those words again and again, and he had made it a principle of his marriage.

More than anything else our homes need the transmitting of love—by word, by look, by gesture, by touch—by all the communicative acts we know.

Closing the Gaps

Two people who love each other sense no communications gaps. A parent may face a generation gap with a child, but it need not be a love gap. Husband and wife may bring differing cultures and education together and still prosper in love.

Love throws a bridge over troubled waters and walks two people toward each other. Love heals rifts between fathers and sons, mothers and daughters. You see, love-as-a-principle has God's power on its side. Every time it operates, it draws God into the relationship, because God is love (love-as-a-principle).

The modern family involves itself in many things. Yet "beneath all the nonsense of the backyard barbecue, the dancing lessons, the crazy commuting—as beneath the earlier nonsense of saving withered roses or the beloved's tears captured in little bottles—that reality of growing together into a whole that is greater than the sum of its parts has sustained and will sustain the ancient institution that has given its form to almost every social arrangement man has known."—*The Sunday Star,* Washington, D.C., January 9, 1972.

We should think carefully about what we want the end result of the family to be. It's not enough to drift on cloud nine—no matter how long the ride lasts. Principles must undergird the family to ensure success.

Most marriages founder on one of several factors, for example, the discipline of children, unfaithfulness, money, relatives.

"I propose that in today's world our homes must stand for at least two things. They must be a place where young people learn the satisfactions of a disciplined way of life and the satisfactions of work well done. . . . When America is increasingly worried by drug habits and drink habits and food habits, let the families in Christian homes develop the work habit as one way of bringing the entire family into closer relationship."—"The Vanishing American Family," *Gleaner,* February 7, 1972, p. 7.

Wherever gaps grow, inadequate communication dwells at their root. Determining principles of family discipline beforehand and sticking to them in support of each other provide one basic way to hold the family together. Extending love within the home so that each partner feels secure and wanted, complete and whole, protects the home against unfaithfulness. Understanding clearly the financial basis undergirding the home results from explanation, cooperation, and, at times, sacrifice of personal wishes.

Roles in the Home

No longer is it enough for the husband to be just Mr. "Law-and-order," or mother to be only tenderness and protection. But their entire roles, carefully defined and understood, help the family survive the storms of changing society.

THREE-WAY TRANSMITTER COMPLEX

Today's father and husband faces complexities that a previous generation could not envision. His position as breadwinner draws him away from the home and especially his children. He goes off to an office or a job which children and sometimes even his wife understand poorly. His work isolates him from the family and even exhausts him so that he cannot enjoy them. Additional pressures from business, community, church, school, and club overwhelm him. Today's mobile society may actually keep him from the family for longer periods than he is with it. The wife develops patterns of life alien to her husband, and so do the children.

Perhaps this is why Ellen White emphasized country living as a desirable state. It has less distractions, less pressures. We should not, however, equate country living with city-fringe living where long commuting distances may hold families apart for even greater periods of time. She is talking of the small farm or a life in the country with easy access to work, but where the pressures and temptations of the city do not intrude.

As troublesome as the role of the father may be, mother and wife faces demands just as complex. Dishwashers and laundromats have brought relief from drudgery, but society expects more of her than just work. The telephone has replaced the back fence, and, if she has small children, it may provide her only contact with friends. Her husband's work may demand development of education and social graces. As he grows more successful, he recedes more and more from her life. When children grow older she becomes a car-pool driver and scoutmaster. To break the boredom of an empty house, she takes on a career or becomes a clubwoman.

As responsibilities change with the times, couples contemplating marriage need to define carefully the roles and relationships their marriages need to survive. They must answer such questions as when and if to bring children into the family, and how many. How will children affect their careers? What if the wife's career eclipses her husband's in income and prestige? How will the husband's work affect the wife and

115

children? How can they maintain contact with God? Will the wife interrupt her career when children arrive? How can both use their talents to most successfully serve the home, the community, and God?

Love faces all such problems and finds solutions according to God's will. But without Christ, without the willingness to sacrifice—to submit self to the good of the family, to take an amended role—the home may fracture. That's why Christ must be the partner of every Christian home.

In Ellen White's time few of her contemporaries faced the problems we know. Yet she herself was a working mother, often separated by her toils from her children. Despite this, she offers an example of successful motherhood. She lists many principles for the home. Among them:

1. The marriage tie is sacred, and partners should strive to develop its strength.

2. Husbands adopt the role of partners, not lords. They must represent a Christlike influence in the home.

3. Each partner should have the opportunity to develop and live a well-rounded life. A mother should never be a drudge.

4. When children enter the home, they become its prime responsibility, and their training and salvation the constant concern of father and mother.

For a shorter survey of Christian principles of homemaking we suggest *Happiness Homemade,* or for more detail, the three books *Child Guidance, The Adventist Home,* and *Messages to Young People,* all by Ellen G. White.

"Happy, Happy Home"

How many of our children have lisped, "With Jesus in the family, Happy, happy home"?

How does Christ enter the home? Ideally He comes to enrich the courtship of young people planning marriage. He becomes the spiritual factor that controls and cements the physical and mental attraction.

116

"Hearts that are filled with the love of Christ can never get very far apart. Religion is love, and a Christian home is one where love reigns and finds expression in words and acts of thoughtful kindness and gentle courtesy."—*Testimonies,* Vol. 5, p. 335.

A Christian influence should pervade the home. Almost limitless resources of aids make it possible for parents to inculcate Christianity from the earliest age. Full-color books, records, flannelgraphs, and coloring books offer audio and visual devices that attract, educate, and inform.

Music can communicate Christ from the earliest years. Children need to feel that they make a contribution to music, not just by turning on a stereo or pushing in a tape cartridge, but by participating in actual music making.

Ancient Israel made songs of the commandments of the Lord. The children sang the truth into their hearts. "If it was essential for Moses to embody the commandments in sacred song, so that as they marched in the wilderness, the children could learn to sing the law verse by verse, how essential it is at this time to teach our children God's Word! Let us come up to the help of the Lord, instructing our children to keep the commandments to the letter. Let us do everything in our power to make music in our homes, that God may come in."—*Evangelism,* p. 500.

Acquaintance with the natural world enriches our understanding of God. Besides the traditional walks through the woods, the microscope and telescope, experiments, and books and discussions of God's created world will direct our thoughts heavenward. Even those who live in the densest cities may reach out to God through His world. True, it may take a little imagination and effort but even Harlem and Calcutta can reveal the hand of the Creator.

The greatest resource in bringing Christ into the home is the lives of its members. Marriage partners who love the Lord will probably love each other. As they love Him more, they will love each other more. Parents who love Christ will speak with His love, touch with His love, smile with His love, and sing with His love. Through worship, word, and example, they will draw their family into the embrace of heaven.

What happens when the best of our endeavors fail, and a child falls victim of our disordered society, or a marriage partner disappoints us? All too often we react in bitterness or self-righteousness. Christ could easily have rejected the woman found in adultery. But He forgave and welcomed her back with the words, "Go, and sin no more." And the father rejoiced in the prodigal that returned. Love-as-a-principle is patient, never gives up, is kind. Many parents have lived and loved through crisis after crisis and finally rejoiced in a child won to the Lord. Christlike love is the Christian's ultimate weapon.

Love's Ever-widening Circle

Headlines tell of the mounting tragedy of shattered families. Millions of children come from broken homes. Yet the real, important story does not lie there.

No one shouts the story of the husband who comes home to thank his wife for her love and care. No one measures the influence of a home that welcomes strangers and helps those in need. No one tells the praises of the millions of teen-agers who say, "No, thank you," to all kinds of temptations. One researcher did record the fact that 66 percent of a group of married couples he polled stated that their homes were "very happy." God wasn't wrong when He made the family. The problems came with sin. The way to keep problems out is to let God in.

The Christian home demonstrates the difference between right and wrong. One young person said to me, "What I need is someone to tell me the difference between right and wrong. Nobody seems to know anymore." Our homes must display the Ten Commandments in practice, in operation. Thirteen million children of broken marriages attest to the need of more Christlike parents, more Christian bonds.

"A lamp, however small, if kept steadily burning, may be

118

the means of lighting many other lamps. Our sphere of influence may seem narrow, our ability small, our opportunities few, our acquirements limited; yet wonderful possibilities are ours through a faithful use of the opportunities of our own homes. If we will open our hearts and homes to the divine principles of life we shall become channels for currents of life-giving power. From our homes will flow streams of healing, bringing life and beauty and fruitfulness where now are barrenness and dearth."—*The Ministry of Healing,* p. 355.

In a society with triple-locked doors, peepholes, intercoms at the door, and German shepherd watchdogs, families tend to become more and more isolated from each other. We move in restricted circles of carefully selected friends. Yet aching oceans of loneliness surround us. People cry out for concern and friendship.

Every home needs to commit itself to some who are not close friends, some who need Christ, some who may be emotionally, educationally, or economically deprived. Young people not of our own families need a place away from temptation. "The warmth of a genial welcome, a place at your fireside, a seat at your home table, the privilege of sharing the blessing of the hour of prayer, would to many . . . be like a glimpse of heaven."—*Ibid.,* p. 354.

CHAPTER 11

COMMUNICATION EXPLOSION

"The concept of interaction is central to an understanding of the concept of process in communication. Communication represents an attempt to couple two organisms, to bridge the gap between two individuals through the production and reception of messages which have meanings for both. At best, this is an impossible task. Interactive communication approaches this ideal. . . .

"The goal of interaction is the merger of self and other, a complete ability to anticipate, predict, and behave in accordance with the joint needs of self and other."—David K. Berlo, *The Process of Communication,* pp. 130, 131.

A communication explosion forces more and more communicative attempts on the Christian. Increasingly complex decisions face us as we seek to determine the effect of entering into communication with someone else. Players in the game of life must peer increasingly further into the future to discover the results and the strategy of the satanic opponent.

Choosing the communicative acts that we will permit into our lives should occupy much of our thought. Even letting certain instruments of communication into our homes brings unexpected or unwanted change.

Marshall McLuhan says, "The medium is the message." What he is trying to tell us is that the instruments of communication themselves change society as much as the messages they transmit. Thus, he claims, television has a message for civilization of far greater impact than the drama, commercials, news reports, and sports events it offers. Television by its very nature will alter the society in which we live, just as the inventing of the print media transformed the world after Gutenberg. The same is true for each of the other forms of mass media.

The real threat of the electronic society isn't the vast array of tools which we use to communicate. It centers in the inevitable changes that the tools make. We do not want to be like the Amish and exclude such devices on religious grounds. Even if we did, we could not escape all the changes they make. Yet, if we do not intelligently face their presence and effect, we may lose touch with the world we are trying to save.

Temptations to sin began in Eden. Since then it has always been easier to sin than not to sin. Learning to live Christian lives, to make Christian choices, within the society that change does produce is our responsibility. It may involve excluding certain mass-media devices or messages from our personal experience. On the other hand, if we do not screen them out, nothing we can do will take away from us the alterations and transformations they did produce.

We can do a lot to protect ourselves. For example, we can monitor the messages we receive. We can turn off the television set, avoid the theater, keep bad books out of our homes.

Babel Once More

Our fantastic age of change has thrust a symbolic tower of Babel to the skies. And from that lofty summit man looks down on past ages and considers his superiority. Yet when you look at man rather than the changes he has made in technology, you discover a morally degenerate race. Men speak to each other through film and television with the pictures and words of lust, greed, anger, and hatred. They prey on each other through the telephone and typewriter.

Messages from the tower of man's devising show that the lightning of divine displeasure has already struck it. Confusion reigns everywhere. "But you must realize that in the last days the times will be full of danger. Men will become utterly self-centered, greedy for money, full of big words. They will

THE MEDIA, THE MESSAGE, AND MAN

be proud and contemptuous, without any regard for what their parents taught them. They will be utterly lacking in gratitude, purity and normal human affections. They will be men of unscrupulous speech and have no control of themselves. They will be passionate and unprincipled, treacherous, self-willed and conceited, loving all the time what gives them pleasure instead of loving God. They will maintain a façade of 'religion,' but their conduct will deny its validity." 2 Timothy 3:1-5, Phillips.

Bombarded with unprecedented communications, modern man struggles to maintain his identity and hardly seems to know why he is here or where he is going. Disorientation is a major symptom of our times.

What rules should the Christian apply to the media? We suggest the following guidelines.

1. Is what it is telling us true? "And now, my friends, all that is true, all that is noble, all that is just and pure, all that is lovable and gracious, whatever is excellent and admirable—fill all your thoughts with these things." Philippians 4:8.

2. Is it moral? "Fornication and indecency of any kind, or ruthless greed, must not be so much as mentioned among you, as befits the people of God. No coarse, stupid, or flippant talk; these things are out of place; you should rather be thanking God." Ephesians 5:3, 4.

3. Is its relevancy Christian? "But you, my friends, are not in the dark, that the day should overtake you like a thief. You are all children of light, children of day. We do not belong to night or darkness." "We, who belong to daylight, must keep sober, armed with faith and love." 1 Thessalonians 5:4, 5, 8.

4. Is Christ still with me after I have exposed myself to it? "Put yourself at the disposal of God, as dead men raised to life; yield your bodies to him as implements for doing right; for sin shall no longer be your master, because you are no longer under law, but under the grace of God." Romans 6:13, 14.

5. Does it build faith? "But you, man of God, must shun

122

all this, and pursue justice, piety, fidelity, love, fortitude, and gentleness. Run the great race of faith and take hold of eternal life." 1 Timothy 6:11, 12.

My Brother's Keeper

Perhaps as a church we have not taken enough interest in shaping the media constructively. Because of the evil perpetrated in them, we tend to shun the communications media and their producers. We see the immorality and evil they portray as signs of the end of human time and, in smug self-satisfaction, watch as things slide toward that end. Frequently we show great interest in helping the end product of a degenerate system but do little to aid the system itself.

Is it worth our involvement to try and change the picture? Can we really make a television station shift its policies? Should we support attempts to reduce pornography and obscenity? Or do we have more important things to do as Christians and Seventh-day Adventists?

Perhaps the attitude of Ellen G. White and the denomination to the evils of intemperance could offer a guide to us. We jump into fights to keep liquor away from youth, to reduce the advertising of tobacco, to eliminate drug abuse. Is our concern only to be with evils that produce physical ill effects? Christians might also concern themselves with the immoral and impure. Thus we may reduce the winds of strife blowing through the minds of millions who might yet accept Christ.

We have a right to feel indignant that drugstores sell printed filth, that movie houses thrive on X-rated films, that crime fills hours of prime-time television, that rock music blasts the senses, that children watch endless sequences of questionable cartoons. I am not about to propose that we shift our emphasis as a church. Social activism must not become our prime objective. We must stay with the task of telling the world about Christ's coming. Yet at the same time we have always accepted a clear call to preserve a climate in which we may more successfully do our work.

Here is how one writer sees just one of the media—film. "Citizens under the age of thirty account for the bulk of the Hollywood audience, and if the customers want to buy romantic fantasy, no matter how distorted or corrosive, then that is what you sell them. The most successful movies of the past summer, both at the box office and with the New York critics, have to do with rats, lust, greed, and insects. In each instance the evil in question triumphs over the rickety moral defenses of the few characters who even bother to raise tentative questions of conscience. A cockroach can be a hero, and a woman is nearly always a whore."—Lewis H. Lapham, "What Movies Try to Sell Us," *Harper's Magazine,* November, 1971, p. 106. We have a right to protest against such things.

Communications have made the world interdependent. Yet at the same time we tend to spend less and less time in cementing personal relationships. The gas attendants seem to be new each week, a different sales person appears at the cash register, our neighbors move. As Christians we actually are having progressively less time, on the average, to make personal contacts and witness to friends and neighbors. Yet a community in constant and increasing flux, plus our own involvement in changes, may be one way in which God is providing opportunities for the church to witness.

"The great work now to be accomplished is to bring up the people of God to engage in the work and exert a holy influence. . . . With wisdom, caution, and love, they should labor for the salvation of neighbors and friends. There is too distant a feeling manifested. . . . All should feel that they are their brother's keeper, that they are in a great degree responsible for the souls of those around them."—*Testimonies,* Vol. 1, p. 368.

Those Lonely People

What is television doing to society? We do not know yet. Television conquered America in less than a generation. While we can spot symptoms, we shall not be sure whether we can clearly identify a disease for many years, perhaps for generations. But one of the most disturbing results of television we can spot is a new kind of segregation. Television separates us from reality—we see the world through a camera eye. Although we know much more, we feel less involved. We observe rather than act.

"A new miasma—which no machine before could emit—enshrouds the world of TV. We begin to be so accustomed to this foggy world, so at home and solaced and comforted within and by its blurry edges, that reality itself becomes slightly irritating."—Daniel J. Boorstin, "Television," *Life,* September 10, 1971, p. 39. Copyright 1971 by Daniel J. Boorstin. Used by permission.

Television is a one-way window. We cannot look around the corner to see who else is watching the event portrayed. Nor can we find the preacher or anyone else to edge up beside to ask him what he thinks of it. It creates a new sense of isolation, confinement, and frustration. We cannot even know what fifty million other viewers are thinking in their segregated viewing chambers.

Television viewing is a solitary experience. At a concert you can applaud with thousands of others. At a ball game people yell in unison. Not with television.

"Many admirable features of American life today—the new poignance of our conscience, the wondrous universalizing of our experiences, the sharing of the exotic, the remote, the unexpected—come from television. But they will come to little unless we find new ways to overcome the new provincialism, the new isolation, the new frustrations and the new confusion which come from our new segregation."—*Ibid.*

Real dangers exist that the modern mass media may actually drive church members away from each other and from the church. It can eventually become a wedge splitting us off in units of segregated, isolated experience. Instead we should cherish opportunities for shared church experience. "The wonderful family to belong to" will only stay wonderful

125

if we are willing to consciously develop new ties to it.

Today the church has a fantastic opportunity to provide the excitement of real, shared experience to others. It is the moment to bring the warmth of Christian experience to the lonely, isolated, frustrated. We have the real thing. Let's give to the world our religious experience in vivid Christ-centered playback.

That motivation study that Faith for Today conducted reminded us that the world is full of vast numbers of lonely people. To them the telecast seemed to offer a hand of friendship.

During Mission '72 I preached a series of meetings in a Washington, D.C., church. Once more I found myself involved with people—shared the problems, loneliness, frustrations, and hopes of real people. It was no turn-on, turn-off TV-type drama. No one wrote a plot that sorted it all out for them in sixty minutes. They were living with their loneliness, their problems. And Christ still provides the best and only successful answer to the human malaise.

"All who profess to have a Father in heaven, who they hope will care for them and finally take them to the home He has prepared for them, ought to feel a solemn obligation resting upon them to be friends to the friendless, and fathers to the orphans, to aid the widows, and be of some practical use in this world by benefiting humanity. Many have not viewed these things in a right light. If they live merely for themselves, they will have no greater strength than this calls for."—*Testimonies*, Vol. 2, p. 329.

Join the Movement

The late sixties saw America's youth involving themselves in all kinds of movements for social change. They marched, demonstrated, wrote, even died for their convictions. Mass media played a large part in sparking their involvement.

Involvement is the other side of the coin of the new segregation. People many times commit themselves to causes they inherit from the media. Special-interest groups, radical and conservative minorities, all try to manipulate the media to tell their story, hoping to involve others.

The horror of the starving East Nigerian baby, portrayed in shocking detail by the closeup camera, stirred the conscience of America. As a result we know what the world suffers. How will the Christian deal with it?

We live in an age of decision. The Bible calls it the judgment hour. Ellen G. White tells us that men by the choices they make are symbolically binding themselves in bundles ready for burning. In graphic language the Bible describes the final judgment. Sheep separated from goats, all, small and great, standing before God, the record books opened. And what of the criteria of judgment?

"When I was hungry, you gave me food; when thirsty, you gave me drink; when I was a stranger you took me into your home, when naked you clothed me; when I was ill you came to my help, when in prison you visited me." Matthew 25:35, 36.

Fantastic that God should talk of involvement. In that passage Christ makes no mention of commandments, just involvement. To think that eternal life should balance on a cup of cold water.

We may meet some needs by helping local situations. In Washington, D.C., Wayne Estep, a young Adventist, operates the Gate—a medical and spiritual center where members of the counter culture may come for counsel and practical help. In Ethiopia, Liberia, Ghana, Palau, Korea, Vietnam, Thailand, Japan, I have observed student missionaries and Adventist Volunteer Service Corps workers who have spotted a need and hastened to fill it.

We must not selfishly squander the stewardship of involvement on more beautiful and expensive churches or serving only local needs. "By its necessities a ruined world is drawing forth from us talents of means and of influence, to present to men and women the truth, of which they are in perishing need. And as we heed these calls, by labor and by acts of

127

benevolence, we are assimilated to the image of Him who for our sakes became poor. In bestowing we bless others and thus accumulate true riches."—*Testimonies,* Vol. 9, pp. 253, 254.

The statistician of the General Conference shows figures that point out an alarming trend. For many years giving to overseas causes eclipsed local expenditures. In recent years the lines on the graph have crossed. Local church projects are climbing while mission giving lags. The problem is complex, but the warning is clear—God expects us to involve ourselves with the needy, sick, poor, deprived, and Christless wherever they live.

The Problem Solvers

One would think that out of the vast amount of fiction created for the print, broadcast, film, and live stage media some kind of answers to personal problems would emerge. Yet the opposite seems the trend. More counselors, psychiatrists, psychoanalysts, and personal problem solvers ply their skills than ever. And at the same time a plethora of gurus, religious quacks, palmists, and astrologers wriggle a careful, oracular way through people's personal problems. Escapism gives no lasting answers. In fact it may aggravate problems.

"There is at least one relatively unpublicized area of pollution, that of the mind. It was Isaiah who spoke out against polluters of the mind when he wrote to the children of Judah: 'Ah sinful nation, a people laden with iniquity, a seed of evildoers, children that are corrupters: they have forsaken the Lord, they have provoked the Holy One of Israel unto anger, they are gone away backward.' Isaiah 1:4, K.J.V.

"Isaiah did not spare words; those who corrupted the mind were leading the people backward. So in our day with the growing publication of pornographic books and magazines and the mass of literature produced under the guise of scientific research, we are in a state of mind pollution, being led backward."—*Bookstore Journal,* June, 1970.

A foggy cloud of schmaltzy love and improbable situations rises from the television screen each day. Millions of American housewives make the TV soap opera their daily fare. And at night father and the kids join them in an unending rerun of escapist drama. In the daytime the world moves from one unsatisfactory semiclimax to the next; in the evening the world gets fixed up in thirty minutes at best and two hours at worst.

No wonder reality seems unsatisfactory. You can't mend a family rift in thirty minutes. Or unstitch a divorce in an hour. You don't wipe out big-time crime in ninety minutes. And cowboys gave up setting the world right a hundred years ago.

"Satan is using every means to make crime and debasing vice popular. We cannot walk the streets of our cities without encountering flaring notices of crime presented in some novel, or to be acted at some theater. The mind is educated to familiarity with sin. The course pursued by the base and vile is kept before the people in the periodicals of the day, and everything that can excite passion is brought before them in exciting stories."—*Patriarchs and Prophets*, p. 459.

God has His way of helping man face his problems and solve them. Jesus said, "Come unto me, all ye that labour and are heavy laden, and I will give you rest. Take my yoke upon you, and learn of me; for I am meek and lowly in heart: and ye shall find rest unto your souls." Matthew 11:28, 29, K.J.V.

Last-day Maelstrom

Fishermen off the coast of Scandinavia fear the maelstrom. Currents meeting in the North Sea produce whirlpools of great power. Small vessels caught in the whizzing tide find themselves drawn faster and faster and closer and closer to the center. A black hole sucks the vessel under.

The coasts of the last days are fraught with many dangers for the Christian. A battle for your mind rages constantly. Satanic forces use the mass media as their frontline weapons.

129

The print, broadcast, film, and stage media threaten spirituality. Satan knows he has only a short time remaining. He works with vicious subtlety to lure and destroy the faith of God's followers. Once caught in his sucking vices, the erring believer may find himself pulled under.

"The Scriptures pointing forward to this time declare that Satan will work with all power and 'with all deceivableness of unrighteousness.' . . . His working is plainly revealed by the rapidly increasing darkness, the multitudinous errors, heresies, and delusions of these last days. Not only is Satan leading the world captive, but his deceptions are leavening the professed churches of our Lord Jesus Christ."—*Christ's Object Lessons*, p. 414.

As one reads the Bible and the writings of Ellen G. White, the impression deepens that we dare not desert our characteristic principles and standards. To compromise will court calamity. We are warned that even church leaders may not always adhere to the highest principles. Each one of us must personally ground our faith.

The strength of the personal relationship that each church member develops with God through Bible study, prayer, and witnessing will determine whether he shall stand in the time of trouble. Spiritual cords must reach out to God day by day in ever-increasing numbers until we find ourselves bound inseparably to the God of our salvation. Nothing will separate Christ from His child.

"I have become absolutely convinced that neither death nor life, neither messenger of Heaven nor monarch of earth, neither what happens today nor what may happen tomorrow, neither a power from on high nor a power from below, nor anything else in God's whole world has any power to separate us from the love of God in Christ Jesus our Lord!" Romans 8:38 39, Phillips.

CHAPTER 12

THE CHURCH IN THE GLOBAL VILLAGE

The world of the late twentieth century pulses with a new and exciting rhythm.

Less than a century ago it took months for news to spread across the world. Today radio, television, and other mass media penetrate the outback of the world with the happenings of everywhere. Not too long ago only a few could comprehend the word that did go out. Today radio and television sweep the illiterate into the circle of information.

The print media held sway for five hundred years as the prime sources of information, thought control, and propaganda. They shaped the world, producing a society based on the clear, logical development of thought that the written word encourages.

Today the audio-visual media dominate with increasing authority. In the United States television has eclipsed newspapers as the prime source of current news.

Late in 1968, as the astronauts probed for the moon, I was holding religious meetings in Shillong, the capital of Assam, the northeastern state of India. We visited our academy out from the town and on the way back wondered how things were going with the space adventurers. Back in Shillong, missionary Ron Baird not only tuned us to shortwave transmissions giving all the details of the historic voyage, but also produced a local paper that contained cabled pictures.

"We live in a new communications environment—a world conditioned by radio, television, the print media, pictures, films, eye-catching signs and displays, and the enchantment—sometimes the agony—of amplified sound. This is the world into which our children are born and raised. It is strange

131

to older folks, but it is the native air of newer generations. It is global. It presses in on persons of all ages, everywhere."—James E. McEldowney, "Christian Communication," *World Association for Christian Communication Journal,* 1971, p. 47.

Twenty-five years ago it was relatively easy to define Christian communication. The church had done it in much the same way since the time of Christ. Today the church would reply with many voices. The preacher, the evangelist, the social worker, would have their concepts of Christian communication. So would the theologian, the Bible scholar, and the Christian educator. Historians, psychologists, or sociologists each have their own glasses with which they peer at the world of communication. And the word from professional broadcasters, film producers, journalist, or artist might yet be different still.

Every life Christ touched responded with a higher note than it had known before. "All who received him, who believed in his name, he gave power to become children of God." John 1:12, R.S.V. Our commission stretches for the same results. The media join us as the technology of the Spirit for our day to help accomplish God's purposes in the earth.

An Impossible Mission?

God has given clear identification to the task of the church. Its message—the Good News of salvation through Christ. Its scope—"every nation, and kindred, and tongue, and people." Its purpose—to prepare a people for the Lord. Its goal—a finished task within "this generation." Its methods—"ye shall receive power, after that the Holy Ghost is come upon you."

Never before has the church had the potential to accomplish things so quickly.

In a special sense the Adventist message is a development of the media. When Gutenberg perfected movable type, he set in motion the possibility of Advent Truth. Up till that time the Word of God resided in rare, expensive manuscripts, or in the hearts of a few who really understood it. Neither Wycliffe nor Huss had the media available to give their message solidifying power or permanence. When the possessors of Biblical truth died or were killed, the movement they fostered disintegrated. But the print media changed all that. Suddenly men could produce a cheap, easily distributed presentation of religious truth.

Though not everyone was literate, yet the impact of the tracts, pamphlets, and copies of Scripture that flowed from the Reformers was wide and lasting. The print media formed a solid core of fact, a point of reference to which people might come and on which they might build further truth. As much as anything else, the printed page overwhelmed the Catholic Church of the sixteenth and seventeenth centuries.

And once wide-ranging minds sensed the goal of truth, they homed on it stage by stage. Interesting parallels exist between the growing expertise of printing and the timing of the three angels' messages. About the time that God released His final message to the world, men were developing the first of the high-speed presses.

Yet one might contemplate the frustration of a worldwide mission hampered by a print-oriented ministry that skips the vast millions of illiterates. And remember it is the illiterates who are providing the present population explosion.

God times with precision. Not long after the first Seventh-day Adventist missionaries left North America, the first radio signals began spanning increasingly large distances. As the organization of the church developed, radio opened new possibilities, until today a growing church faces the tantalizing possibility that it can really reach all men everywhere with the Word.

An impossible mission? Not now. Not any longer. Now it can be done.

"God has called this people to give to the world the message of Christ's soon coming. We are to give to men the last call to the gospel feast, the last invitation to the marriage supper of the Lamb. Thousands of places that have not heard the call are yet to hear it. Many who have not given the message are yet to proclaim it."—*Testimonies*, Vol. 6, p. 412.

Matching the Times

My small portable radio has a shortwave band. Once, in the highlands of New Guinea, I spent an interesting half hour ascertaining what was reaching that emerging nation. In my exploration I found one particularly powerful signal. For a few minutes I listened to clean, crisp English. Obviously the speaker had training from one of the British universities. He was talking to the people of New Guinea. The voice belonged to Radio Peking. Its vocabulary was so high over the heads of the vast majority of New Guineans that it had lost any hope of true communication with the people. Yet I remember asking myself, "What will happen when they discover pidgin English?"

In giving the message of the three angels, God hit square in the center of twentieth-century problems and concepts. Into a world where so-called Christian theologians proclaim a theology with a dead god, a Christianity without a Christ, a morality without standards, and a creation without a Creator, enters a command to return to the transcendent God, the personal Creator.

Who is Babylon? Let us not confine the "confusion" of the last days alone to the great religiopolitical apostasy—as widespread and potent as that might be. Let us see the arch-deceiver as the master of all confusion. He is at work in everything that substitutes for truth. All the assaults on God's revelation, God's people, and God's character are Babylon.

We need the power of the mass media to help overcome error. How easy to condemn the media as devil-ridden, evil orifices of seduction, yet they are one of God's ways of finishing the church's mission. They may yet, as the angels at Christ's birth, proclaim the Good News to a dying world.

So many cry for deliverance. People want escape from sin,

from suffering, from poor health, from poverty, from inequality, from injustice. And there is deliverance. "And it shall come to pass, that whosoever shall call on the name of the Lord shall be delivered: for in mount Zion and in Jerusalem shall be deliverance, as the Lord hath said, and in the remnant whom the Lord shall call." Joel 2:32, K.J.V.

Our message gives deliverance. As a people of prophecy we proclaim deliverance. Look at the Book of Daniel—a book specifically written to confirm God as the Deliverer.

Daniel 1: God delivers from poor health habits.

Daniel 2: God proclaims Himself as the Controller of human destiny, who will deliver through intervention.

Daniel 3: We have our first direct look at Christ the Deliverer as He steps into the furnace of trial to deliver the three Israelites.

Daniel 4: A mad monarch finds that even his pride-induced psychoses yield to the Deliverer.

Daniel 7: Christ appears in judgment to declare deliverance for His people and consume the servitude of apostasy.

Daniel 9: Christ as Messiah delivers from sin and transgression.

Daniel 12: Michael delivers those whose "names are written."

Technology of the Spirit

God speaks of a remnant, of a special group who will proclaim His messages in the final days of human history. At this moment God has nearly four billion people alive that Christ died to save. How many will He save? We do not know, neither can we compute. John does speak of "a great multitude, which no man could number," but we must look for a remnant in quality of belief, not quantity of people.

How would God save this group of people? Through the technology of the Spirit.

At Pentecost God had no printing presses to pass the word of the risen Christ. Mount Zion boasted no tall transmitting towers. God sent the Holy Spirit to multiply what He did possess. In a fantastic personal infilling, God provided thrust and power that took the Good News to the corners of the Roman Empire and beyond by A.D. 100. The speed and conquests of early Christianity eclipse anything the modern church has experienced. Man is God's first and best technology. Whatever has happened since has only added new tools to the inventory of the Spirit as He works through man to accomplish divine purposes.

The technology of the Spirit takes an editor, a journalist, an author, an evangelist, and turns a printing press into Pentecost talking in the thousands of languages of the world. The technology of the Spirit takes a broadcaster, an engineer, a scriptwriter, a producer, and turns transmitters and film stock into the Good News blanketing the continents and spanning the seas.

James J. Aitken, former world leader for radio and television for Seventh-day Adventists, says that the church needs apostles of the media—men and women who burn to let the Spirit use them through radio, television, film, print, audiovisuals. Such men we have already seen—H. M. S. Richards, H. M. S. Richards, Jr., W. A. Fagal, George E. Vandeman, to mention a few in North America; and L. C. Naden, B. F. Perez, Roberto Rabello, to focus on a few in other countries.

Yet we are scarcely touching what we might accomplish. Los Angeles has more than sixty radio stations—every one with an audience, usually faithful and hard to shift. We ought to be asking ourselves, How can the Adventist message speak through each station to its listeners. And we ought to be framing similar questions about television, the print media, film, and every other new method God created for the Spirit to use.

If we are to take anything from the "increase of knowledge" and rapid transit of the last days, it is that we must use them to spread the knowledge of God's Word, that we must hasten about with Biblical truth. It is not enough to stand in awe of flights to the moon. We should be grasping for the same communications technology that made them possible and employ it to prepare men for the flight to heaven.

"We have no time to lose; God calls upon us to watch for souls as they that must give an account. Advance new principles, and crowd in the clear-cut truth."—*Testimonies to Ministers*, p. 118.

The Beautiful Feet

Yet it is not enough to stride with radio's seven-league boots to the ends of the earth. As the Holy Spirit's tools we must find, meet, persuade, and baptize individuals. People-to-people communication alone accomplishes such tasks.

Writes one Christian communicator: "Church lost its ability to communicate with the society at large because of its inability to make the transition from a simple print oriented society with a small educated elite to a pluralistic society where electronic mass media have persuasive influence.

"Church has to capture the fact that it is most influential on a local level and service it with resources that deal with local realities. In order to survive as a viable organization during the last half of this century, the American church must dynamically acknowledge their persistent trend toward localization. Denominations must see themselves more in the role of resources and less in the role of a packager of programming that local churches are honor-bound to carry out."—William K. Waterston, "The Communications Gap," *World Association for Christian Communication Journal*, 1971, pp. 28, 29.

Our evangelists are finding that people do not so much demand a series of proof-texts prepared by denominational headquarters in order to accept the truth, but rather a confrontation—a relationship—with the Christ such as the evangelist knows. Many people find relevant only what they have personally experienced. Yes, they will need doctrinal proofs, but more than that, they want to know what Jesus can and has done for them.

God is searching for what Isaiah calls the beautiful feet of those who will take Christ to the world. A tremendous need exists. Statistics compiled for North America by the Radio and Television Department of the General Conference reveal that less than 50 percent of the names of interested people sent by the Voice of Prophecy and Faith for Today ever receive visits by local representatives.

God taught us a great lesson about evangelism when He sent Jesus Christ. Only in and through a Life could man comprehend God. And only in a life changed by the Life can the world grasp and understand God today.

"The gospel is to be presented, not as a lifeless theory, but as a living force to change the life. God desires that the receivers of His grace shall be witnesses to its power. Those whose course has been most offensive to Him He freely accepts; when they repent, He imparts to them His divine Spirit, places them in the highest positions of trust, and sends them forth into the camp of the disloyal to proclaim His boundless mercy. He would have His servants bear testimony to the fact that through His grace men may possess Christ-likeness of character, and may rejoice in the assurance of His great love. He would have us bear testimony to the fact that He cannot be satisfied until the human race are reclaimed and reinstated in the holy privileges as His sons and daughters."—*The Desire of Ages,* p. 826.

We speak through mass media to the people in the global village. Yet God must also have His runners who will carry the message in person, seeking those who heard, and those who would hear, and bringing saving hope to them.

Actors in the Divine Drama

Perhaps Shakespeare was echoing Paul's concepts when he said, "All the world's a stage." God says that He has put the church on the world stage to demonstrate what He has accomplished with man through Christ.

Some students of human psychology have suggested that

the television camera brought the student protests of the late sixties in North America. Riot, violence, and bizarre dress attracted television crews and became a method of proclaiming the radical ethic. A consciousness of being continually "on camera" may provoke different styles of dress. Hippies confess to adopting nonconformist styles as much to show the role they are playing as to protest the "establishment."

For the church the development of mass media is changing concepts, too. No longer may we successfully hold double standards. What we do in North America will become known to the ends of the earth, and vice versa. An isolated indiscretion, discrimination, or inconsistency may quickly become accepted as the norm if given wide publicity.

In recent years church members overseas have become increasingly aware of the affluence of the church and its members in countries like America, Canada, and Australia. We know of the poverty of the developing world, they know of the riches of the developed world. Such knowledge puts our use of wealth to a test.

A sense of family binds the Advent Movement together. When something bad happens within the family, we try to cover it up. We do not want the world to know about it. Again, we realize the importance the impressions the lives of the saints can make. David states that God shines out of Zion, the perfection of beauty. (Psalm 50:2.) Just as nothing testifies more to the success of a parent than the life of a son or daughter, so nothing reflects better the glory of God than the mirror of a character polished in the image of Christ. What God can do with fallen humanity is one of His greatest glories.

"The faces of men and women who walk and work with God express the peace of heaven. They are surrounded with the atmosphere of heaven. For these souls the kingdom of God has begun. They have Christ's joy, the joy of being a blessing to humanity. They have the honor of being accepted for the Master's use; they are trusted to do His work in His name."—*Ibid.*, p. 312.

139

To Every Man's Door

"You possess full knowledge and you can give full expression to it, because in you the evidence for the truth of Christ has found confirmation. There is indeed no single gift you lack, while you wait expectantly for our Lord Jesus Christ to reveal himself." 1 Corinthians 1:5-7.

A modern Paul might also write similarly of Seventh-day Adventists today. God pours out His blessings. A developing core of resources and talent has matched a developing technology to aid the mission of the church.

No way existed for our first missionaries to reach all the world. Vast populations wait behind doors locked fast through ignorance, illiteracy, or lack of personnel. God almost seems to be saying to us, "I know you cannot put someone in every village in India where you have scarcely more than one member for every ten villages. I know they are locking the entranceways to apartment towers in New York, Chicago, and Tokyo. I know you can't get in. So I create a new tool, a new way to challenge your faith. My gifts, My technology, will always keep pace with your needs. You will not lack in any gift."

New tools are coming into the inventory of Christian workers. Right now a church in California tapes its service and then delivers it to interested people who see it played back that afternoon by videotape cassette. Currently you can buy videotape and a player that will project full-color images on your television screen. Think of a lay evangelist equipped with such a tool.

Cable television is wiring the nation for new developments in communications. By the year 1980 communications experts expect that multiple cable facilities will offer minority and special-interest groups opportunities to present their messages by television at modest cost. It will become as easy for an evangelist to rent a cable as it is for him to rent a hall. And he will know exactly whose home is wired for that cable.

140

God will not fail to see that someone or something carries His word to every man's door. Machines of the future might permit us to deliver tracts and magazines via home news and entertainment centers right into the living rooms of the world. "Fax" (for facsimile) machines could give printouts of news, information, and, incidentally, the Good News, right into the waiting hands of millions.

In such ways we may continue to have access to the hearts and homes of men and women. Electronic communication will open doors for person-to-person contact.

Yet, eager Christians find that no doors have really closed. You may not always be able to make personal contact at the door. But in work places, colleges, and streets, opportunities abound for Christian witness.

To fail in personal witness is to fail in the first and foremost giving of the Holy Spirit. Pentecost was to help people meet people in Christian witness. God gives Pentecost again and again to His church as members find the mission of witness. Leaving the spreading of the gospel to print, tape, or film is to fail to capture their purpose. The technology of the Spirit is witness. And witness He will, whether we aid Him or not, until He finishes His work of conviction and guiding. "The world is out of joint. As we look at the picture, the outlook seems discouraging. But Christ greets with hopeful assurance the very men and women who cause us discouragement. In them He sees qualifications that will enable them to take a place in His vineyard. If they will constantly be learners, through His providence He will make them men and women fitted to do a work that is not beyond their capabilities; through the impartation of the Holy Spirit He will give them power of utterance."—*Testimonies*, Vol. 7, p. 271.

CHAPTER 13

READ BY ALL MEN

"The badge of Christianity is not an outward sign, not the wearing of a cross or a crown, but it is that which reveals the union of man with God. By the power of His grace manifested in the transformation of character the world is to be convinced that God has sent His Son as its Redeemer. No other influence that can surround the human soul has such power as the influence of an unselfish life. The strongest argument in favor of the gospel is a loving and lovable Christian."—*The Ministry of Healing*, p. 470.

When my wife and I transferred from New Zealand to America, we wondered what the children would wear to school. Like many other countries, New Zealand schools, both Adventist and state, require that students dress in uniforms. We could not imagine how we could provide all the clothes that a nonuniform situation would demand, or how we could avoid the problems of dress competition. We finally solved them on the spot in Takoma Park—at least partially.

School systems which insist on uniforms do so to encourage a sense of pride in the school, to provide a method of identifying children going to and from school, to help with neatness, and to maintain discipline. A uniform communicates to everybody who you are.

When God called Israel, He gave them specific instructions about dress. "The Lord spoke to Moses and said, Speak to the Israelites in these words: You must make tassels like flowers on the corners of your garments, you and your children's children. Into this tassel you shall work a violet thread, and whenever you see this in the tassel, you shall remember all the Lord's commands and obey them, and not go your own wanton ways, led astray by your own eyes and hearts. This token is to ensure that you remember all my commands and obey them, and keep yourselves holy, consecrated to your God." Numbers 15:37-40.

Then, as now, God wanted His people to communicate to themselves and to the world their identity. Though He no longer requires a visible sign that indicates loyalties, the Christian will communicate God's love in his heart just as tangibly as the Israelites did.

Signals of the Divine Life Within

What condition communicates Christ best? Jesus summed up the principles of Christian character in the Beatitudes.

"How blest are those who know their need of God," He said. Only as we recognize our need can the formation of godly character take place. A sense of lack makes us want God to put us right through Christ. No false sense of personal esteem survives a confrontation with the holiness of Christ.

Instead we share the experience of those who are among "the sorrowful," repenting of our sins and grasping for the righteousness of Christ. Already clearer signals begin to emanate from the life—signals undistorted by sin. When we know our need of God, when we are spiritually sorrowful, we develop a "gentle spirit." Great power lies in meekness. Only those of a gentle spirit may rule in the kingdom of God. Such a spirit shouts the victory of Christ over sin.

Concern fills the life which sees so many on the wrong way. "How blest are those who hunger and thirst to see right prevail." Such concern puts missionaries in the Andes, pilots over Sarawak, laymen in the homes of their friends. Yet in striving to let "right prevail," the Christian uses no force except love. "Those who show mercy" do not need the force of arms or propaganda. They avoid criticism or gossip, they live and practice the Golden Rule.

Such people reflect a purity of life that attracts others. "Those whose hearts are pure" not only "see God," but they

143

permit others to "see God." Thus they become "the peace-makers," bringing peace from Christ to those troubled and perplexed. They become "his sons," increasing the adopted family of God and bringing the same status to others through their peacemaking role. And so the cycle begins again in other lives. (Matthew 5:3-9.)

Christ said that such people become the flavoring of the world—the salt of the earth.

Heather, like many two-year-olds, loved to explore the world with fingers and mouth. One evening at worship her father distributed tightly rolled slips of paper containing Bible promises from what the family called the promise box. Heather wanted one. But when the family turned to her and her father reached for the promise, she promptly put it in her mouth. Retrieving the soggy strip of paper, her father read, "O taste and see that the Lord is good."

The lives of Christians stand like beacons on a hill. Pilots flying across the landscape determine their position by fixed radio beams that radiate out from airports. By triangulation the fliers determine exactly where they are. The Christian also lights a homing path for every wayfarer to follow through a dark world.

The church can tolerate no false beacons. Who can count the importance of a life lived in harmony with divine truth? As night fell in the Australian Alps, the stars sprinkled the velvet night with diamonds. We felt secure in our hut. But morning found all trails obliterated by a summer snowstorm. We could determine our destination only by the use of a compass. After careful map reading and sighting of mountain peaks, we set out by compass bearing. At one stage fog closed in. But the small instrument and the maps proved accurate. Finally we topped a ridge twenty miles along the trail and found ourselves right on course.

For millions of souls a Christian neighbor or workmate may be the only compass, the only beacon they ever see to point them to eternal life. And it will be the one that most people will put their greatest confidence in.

144

What Shall I Say?

God equips all His children with a message and methods to use it. No follower of Christ will ever lack a word of witness or a way to witness. "You will receive power when the Holy Spirit comes upon you; and you will bear witness for me in Jerusalem, and all over Judaea and Samaria, and away to the ends of the earth." Acts 1:8.

When Plato reported Socrates' discourse that led the wise man to decide in favor of the existence of God, he displayed an admirable sequence of syllogisms. One reason the church of the middle ages went off the track was their search for logic to support the idea of God's existence. They patterned themselves after the Greek way of thinking, not the Hebrew. Following Greek logic to an extreme, they found themselves disputing the size of angels and how many could dance on a pinpoint. They even tried to compute the weight of an immovable object that would confound an omnipotent God. If they had followed the Hebrew way of knowing God, they would have sought Him through experience, not the Greek approach of reasoning God out.

No wonder God said, "I will render double unto thee; when I have bent Judah for me, filled the bow with Ephraim, and raised up thy sons, O Zion, against thy sons, O Greece, and made thee as the sword of a mighty man." Zechariah 9:12, 13, K.J.V. Paul said, "The Greeks seek after wisdom." 1 Corinthians 1:22, K.J.V. While we must not discount logic or rational thinking as an aid to finding God, we know Him best through personal experience. Both Greek and Jew make their contribution to knowledge. But in the knowledge of God the Jew comes closer with his assertion that any man may experience God.

And such experience infects others. Peter spread the Jesus contagion to the poor physical wreck by the Temple gate. Consider the power of the name of Jesus. One moment the cripple had thoughts only of money. Then the apostles spoke

145

the name of Jesus, and a miracle occurred. God healed the man's physical infirmity.

In the moment of the miracle, did the beggar remember Jesus the healer? Did he perhaps recall vain attempts to get near the Master? Whatever happened, Peter's faith snapped eternal life into him like a light turns on.

You see, a Christian's faith has creative power. Like a powerful current, it sets a sinful life aglow with faith. Faith creates more faith. Peter's faith in Christ produced faith in the heart of the cripple. Then the healed cripple crackled with the electricity of faith. He leaped, walked, ran, praised God.

What equipment do you need to witness? First and foremost, you need your own personal experience. The more you enrich that, the better you communicate Christ.

"But if this faith does not provoke to good works, and lead those who profess it to imitate the self-denying life of Christ, Satan is not disturbed; for they merely assume the Christian name, while their hearts are still carnal, and he can use them in his service even better than if they made no profession. Hiding their deformity under the name of Christian, they pass along with their unsanctified natures, and their evil passions unsubdued. This gives occasion for the unbeliever to reproach Christ with their imperfections, and causes those who do possess pure and undefiled religion to be brought into disrepute."—Ellen G. White, *Early Writings*, p. 227.

Clean Signals

We sometimes forget how wide the communicative media stretch. Not just in the media of radio, print, and television, but in the way we dress, the smile we share, the way we walk, and in every detail of life we communicate. A message supported by true Christian living carries the full punch of the Good News.

All of us must talk, at some time, about our faith. Understanding the Bible and its teachings fits us to tell about God. "We need to search the Scriptures as never before. The Word of God is to be our educator, our guide. We are to understand what saith the Scriptures. . . . We have a grand and solemn work to do, for the world is to be enlightened in regard to the times in which we live; and they will be enlightened when a straight testimony is borne."—Ellen G. White in *S.D.A. Bible Commentary*, Vol. 3, p. 1146.

Though we speak the truth with love, no one should ever doubt what the truth is. Sound Christians develop from a study of the Word. When a person has only a superficial knowledge of the Bible, he suffers at the hands of the unscrupulous who can twist him into error.

Hezekiah told the truth about his wealth, but he failed to relate it to the One who made it possible. Self subtracts clarity from the signals we emit. And self exhibits itself in many ways. We show it in pride, in selfish greed, in anger, hate, covetousness. And we show it in dress, in the priorities of life that we set, in self-pity.

A few years ago we were installing professional recording equipment in our church's studios in Sydney, Australia. When we finally got everything wired, we began our tests. Immediately we picked up a hum—perhaps the most annoying of all electronic hitches. Hours of tedious testing and searching followed. Everything seemed in order. Then one final, seemingly foolish check revealed the problem. We opened the back of one of the machines and found that the ground wire had come loose from the amplifier chassis.

The context and culture of the passage speak of a different type of symbolism, yet it applies aptly: "That Christ may dwell in your hearts by faith; that ye, being rooted and grounded in love, . . . may be able . . . to know the love of Christ." Ephesians 3:17-19, K.J.V. For the signals of faith to come through loud and clear, the Christian must be "grounded" in love.

"This union with Christ, once formed, must be maintained. . . . This is no casual touch, no off-and-on connection.

147

. . . The life you have received from Me can be preserved only by continual communion. Without Me you cannot overcome one sin, or resist one temptation."—*The Desires of Ages,* p. 676.

"The whole work of grace is one continual service of love, or self-denying, self-sacrificing effort. During every hour of Christ's sojourn upon the earth, the love of God was flowing from Him in irrepressible streams. All who are imbued with His Spirit will love as He loved."—*Ibid.,* pp. 677, 678.

Clear Channels

God takes the simplest ideas and turns them into a flood of good. In 1960 Ernest H. J. Steed, then Public Relations Secretary for the Australasian Division, invited me to cooperate in launching the world's first Dial-a-Prayer. He did all the organizing and promotion, I simply provided the voice.

We installed one telephone-answering machine in the Division office. I put a sample message on it. Pastor Steed left for New Guinea. Within a few days, simply by word of mouth from the Division staff, the machine was flooded with calls.

Then a newspaper called about it. Television got the word. On one day three television crews called at the office and took pictures, asked questions, recorded the prayers. Radio gave national coverage.

The telephone exchange went crazy. Calls jumped to open circuits. One realtor received more than forty requests for prayer. Calls came in at the rate of about one every second, but the machine would accept one only every eighty seconds. Telephone company officials pleaded with us to stop the machine. The hunger for spiritual help threatened the entire telephone service of the North Shore of Sydney.

Two months later we started again—with seven machines!

Men and women are waiting to make contact with God. They grasp at small hopes to find faith. What could we offer them better than a clear channel between us and them, and between us and God?

Christians frequently get uptight about standards. Arguments go on and on about dress lengths, hair lengths, jewelry, makeup, and so on. The Bible advises, though, "Women again must dress in becoming manner, modestly and soberly, not with elaborate hair-styles, not decked out with gold or pearls, or expensive clothes, but with good deeds, as befits women who claim to be religious." 1 Timothy 2:9. "Your beauty should reside, not in outward adornment—the braiding of the hair, or jewelry, or dress—but in the inmost centre of your being, with its imperishable ornament, a gentle, quiet spirit, which is of high value in the sight of God." 1 Peter 3: 3, 4.

Why should the Christian follow such standards? So that self-pride may die and Christ flow through.

We see a woman dress a certain way, and we categorize her. Youth come under scrutiny, and adults, sometimes foolishly, group them according to how they dress. The Bible and the writings of Ellen G. White plead with us to avoid extremes. The cost of expensive clothing, hairdos, and jewelry could bless the work of God. Yet that is not the most important factor. What we wear and how we wear it may actually block the signals of Christ from within the life.

Power lies latent in many a life. Gospel power radiates stronger and stronger as we use it. Too often we shield the power. God says, Let it out. Don't bottle up the Good News.

"Everyone on whom is shining the light of present truth is to be stirred with compassion for those who are in darkness. From all believers, light is to be reflected in clear, distinct rays. A work similar to that which the Lord did through His delegated messengers after the Day of Pentecost He is waiting to do today. At this time, when the end of all things is at hand, should not the zeal of the church exceed even that of the early church? Zeal for the glory of God moved the disciples to bear witness to the truth with mighty power. . . . Should not the power of God be even more mightily revealed today than in the time of the apostles?"—*Testimonies,* Vol. 7, p. 33.

Receiving the Word

God delivers to His people the responsibility of warning the world. "Never was there greater need of faithful warnings and reproofs, and close, straight dealing, than at this very time. Satan has come down with great power, knowing that his time is short. He is flooding the world with pleasing fables."— *Ibid.*, Vol. 3, p. 327.

While the gospel rings with positive notes, it also shouts of danger ahead. We should hedge our friends and neighbors about with tactful, persistent reminders of the times in which we live and what they mean. Failure to warn delays the return of Christ.

"If every soldier of Christ had done his duty, if every watchman on the walls of Zion had given the trumpet a certain sound, the world might ere this have heard the message of warning. But the work is years behind. While men have slept, Satan has stolen a march upon us."—*Ibid.*, Vol. 9, p. 29.

Noah preached righteousness and warned a world. One man did that. Could there yet be Noahs sleeping within our churches today, unconscious of responsibility or potential?

What is our message of warning? Once people lived in dread of hellfire. Ours is not to be a message of fear. "We must endeavor to present the truth as the people are prepared to hear it and to appreciate its value. The Spirit of God is working upon the minds and hearts of men, and we are to work in harmony with it."—*Ibid.*, Vol. 6, p. 55.

No doubt should linger as to the content of God's communication to earth's last human age. "And I saw another angel fly in the midst of heaven, having the everlasting gospel to preach unto them that dwell on the earth, and to every nation, and kindred, and tongue, and people." Revelation 14:6, K.J.V. "The messages of this chapter [Revelation 14] constitute a threefold warning, which is to prepare the inhabitants of the earth for the Lord's second coming."—*The Great Controversy*, p. 435.

150

We know the statement's truth. More than 2,000,000 have accepted God's message. God's communication is effective and will yet be more effective. The sowing of over 120 years of witness and warning will produce a great harvest.

The evangelism of the world involves vast numbers. One converted person may carry the gospel to thousands of others. Thousands we can reach in the most simple of ways. Thousands of cities face impending destruction. God will use thousands of common people in missionary activities. More than a thousand people will soon be converted in one day. Thousands of people in the cities have not yet bowed the knee to Baal. Thousands of families will have God's people visit them. (For additional information see: *Evangelism*, pp. 443, 693; *The Adventist Home*, p. 136; *Education*, pp. 269-271; *S.D.A. Bible Commentary*, Vol. 2, p. 1035; *Testimonies*, Vol. 9, p. 126.)

The church's mission will soon explode with success. We are inching through the door of opportunity when we should be bursting it wide open. God wants to lighten the world with His glory. And we are His only way of doing it.

Seven Day Communication

South of Bunbury in Western Australia two Seventh-day Adventist families carved homesteads out of the eucalypt forest. Desperate for companionship, they hacked a road for thirteen miles between their homes. Then each Friday they would trek the distance by bullock wagon to share fellowship. Later settlers distorted the denominational name. Today the local government has paved the track and the signpost calls it "Seven Day Road."

No last-day Christian dares walk any road but the seven day road. Christ must live within every day, every hour, every moment.

One Sabbath afternoon, at a youth camp, a group of us headed off into the Australian bush to look at the beauties around us. Nature shed its lavishness in the purple bark of eucalypts, the fragrance of sun orchids, the warm buzz of bush bees, the crackle of lizards and tiny creatures racing from our path.

One delight led to another until someone said to me, "Pastor Scragg, shouldn't we head back?" Only then did I realize that I was in charge. And we were lost. Long before we stumbled on any path, night fell. We clambered down the cliffs to a stream that led back to the river where the camp lay.

Following the slippery creek bed was arduous. Linking hands, we tripped and fell together. I felt around for the best path, using my feet, shins, hands, and head to detect obstacles ahead. Then one of the chain of young people yelled, "Look, a light!" Yes, it was. One of the campers had come looking for us. Hearing us singing, "My Lord knows the way through the wilderness," he raced through the bush toward us. With the aid of the light, we reached the camp in minutes.

What the world needs is a light. Jesus said, "I am the light of the world." But He also said, "You are light for all the world. . . . When a lamp is lit, it is not put under the meal-tub, but on the lamp-stand, where it gives light to everyone in the house. And you, like the lamp, must shed light among your fellows, so that, when they see the good you do, they may give praise to your Father in heaven." Matthew 5:14-16.

My family and I wound our way up from the warm coolness of the valley. We drove against the setting sun. Then as we rounded a corner, the whole of both sides of the road blazed with brilliant pink. "Look at the flowers!" we chorused. I stopped, and we scrambled out. Looking back, we found the flowers had vanished. We bent to look for them. They were husks of dried grass that had shed their seeds. Lighted with the sun they glowed with beauty. Without the sun they were dismal, dead.

"But unto you that fear my name shall the Sun of righteousness arise with healing in his wings." Malachi 4:2, K.J.V. In this rests the secret of successful Christian communication. Thus it will be in earth's final hours. "And after these things

I saw another angel come down from heaven, having great power; and the earth was lightened with his glory." Revelation 18:1, K.J.V. With the aid of the angel's great power the church will communicate the gospel to all the world. And when all will have listened and responded in one way or other to the gospel, Christ will come and remove all communication barriers between God and man, and between man and man.